Dmitry Artimovich

ONLINE PAYMENT SOLUTIONS

The evolution of Visa and MasterCard

Regulation and development of payment systems in Europe

Table of contents

Author's note

Acknowledgments

INTRODUCTION

PART ONE

1. Background

2. Participants in card payment systems

3. Legislation

4. The Rules of Payment Systems

5. Technical interaction and transaction security

5.1. Key events and turning points that shaped the history of PCI DSS

5.2. Technical integration

6. The risks of Visa & MasterCard payment systems

6.1. Potential risks for cardholders

6.2. Potential risks for acquiring banks

6.3. Potential risks for merchants

PART TWO

Financial system basics

1. Legal Principles

2. Financial institutions

3. Non-banking Financial Institutions (NBFIs)

3.1. Distinctive features of the Russian NBFIs

4. Banks

5. EU rules on payment services

6. Consumer rights

7. Pan-European settlement and payment systems

8. Single Euro Payments Area (SEPA)

9. BASE II Clearing System Basics

10. VisaNet

11. Who can issue banks card in Europe?

12. SWIFT

PART THREE

Visa and MasterCard

1. The Evolution of Payment Systems

1.1. The Evolution of Visa

1.1.1. Part One

1.1.2. Part Two

1.1.3. Part Three

1.1.4. Part Four

1.2. Epilogue

1.3. The Evolution of MasterCard

1.4. Types of Cards

2. Settlement Participants

2.1. Basic concepts

3. The Rules of Payment Systems

3.1. Definitions

3.2. Merchant registration with IPS

3.2.1. MID, TID, GID

3.2.2. MCC

3.2.3. Descriptor

3.2.4. Registration

3.3. Visa Public Rules

3.3.1. General Provisions

3.3.2. Issuer

3.3.3. Acquirer

3.3.4. Merchant

3.3.5. Payment Facilitator

4. Technical integration

4.1. Basic Operations

4.2. Derived operations

4.3. PCI DSS

5. Risks

5.1. Acquirer's Responsibility

5.2. Dispute Resolution.

5.2.1. Chargeback

5.3. Visa chargebacks

5.4. Chargebacks Time Limits.

5.5. 3-D Secure

5.5.1. Early History

5.5.2. Liability Shift

5.6. Fraud Advice

5.7. Visa Chargeback Monitoring Program

5.8. MasterCard Excessive Chargeback Program

5.9. Visa Non-Compliance Assessments

6. The cost of Conducting Internet payments

6.1. Overview

6.2. Transaction Cost

6.3. Interchange Fee

6.4. Industry-specific interchange

6.5. Fees

6.6. Interchange plus

6.7. Surcharge

6.8. Conclusion

PART FOUR

High-Risk Processing

1. History of the term

2. Visa Global Brand Protection Program

3. Visa Rules

3.1. Visa Global Brand Protection Program

3.2. Requirements for all Visa Europe acquirers

3.3. What is High-Brand Risk?

4. Visa Core Rules and Visa Product and Service Rules

5. MasterCard Rules

5.1. Business Risk Assessment and Mitigation (BRAM) Program

Glossary of terms

Author's note

The purpose of this book is to give readers a thorough insight into the international payment systems Visa and MasterCard. Strangely enough, too many professionals in the e-commerce market don't have a clear idea as to how the card payment systems work. You'd find even fewer knowledgeable people in online stores, in fact such are practically never to be met, however, it is in this segment of the market that the "we want it cheaper" kind of demands are routinely voiced in a rather obtrusive manner. I didn't mean to write this book for the satisfaction of those clients who are regularly pleading for significant costs reduction.

This book before you is covering all aspects of the functioning of international payment systems Visa / MasterCard. Perhaps my foremost task in this textbook is to encourage young minds to create new technologies in the field of card payments.

The idea of this textbook was born many years ago, at the time I was working for Chronopay, an electronic payment provider operating in Russia since 2003. In our work we used drafts and blueprints of this book as an introductory instruction to the personnel training manuals. Unfortunately, I could not publish a full textbook while working at the company. All in good time. Now this book is ready for you.

I can't help but draw attention to that specific archness of economic knowledge, for an economist is always forced to pursue two different modes of intellectual activity. Whenever it is necessary to analyze today's actual reality, he always has at his disposal all kinds of facts that are begging to be coherently and consistently expounded. However, when it comes to predicting the future, we're short on facts even for a more or less coherent presentation. In such a situation an economist hastily tries to fill the information gaps with his own theories and hunches based on the analysis of the present-day data. Those of you who have any experience with stock-exchange know well that predicting graph behavior is quite easy, but only up to the present moment, while predictors into the future usually fail.

When facts are lacking researchers face a very different task of meticulously separating the grain from the chaff, while trying to delineate the simplest possible hypothesis that would link all the available facts into a seamless and meaningful whole. On top of that, he is most likely to come up with more that one hypotheses. They do not necessarily have to be true, because, in fact, their only purpose is to put facts in a meaningful order. Then, after comparing all the available hypotheses, there is some probability that the light of truth will be revealed.

Therefore, before we proceed with the study of payment systems, let's try to find a consistent and clear answer to questions concerning the most important economic facts of the twentieth century.

The question that should be addressed early on in any book on money is "What is money?" The answer might seem obvious, however, any economic definitions of money do not stand up to scrutiny. Of course, money is all of the following: a commodity, a measure of exchange, an embodied labor and much more. But not only that. This notorious missing link had for a long time prevented us from formulating a single consistent definition for that "embodied labor".

In the 1930's, the Dutch philosopher Johan Huizinga in his book "Homo Ludens – A study of the play-element in culture" ventured to place play at the core of human existence rather than instincts or economic interest. Such are the facts of life that are becoming more and more obvious. For after all and in the last analysis, what is money?

Money is a convention and its material essence is vanishing before our own eyes with the advent of electronic money, cryptocurrencies, as well as such straightforward phone payments as WeChat and ApplePay. Most transactions are now carried out through computer networks. "Stock-market game" is an established term. The fact that money is virtual and is independent of production processes had always been known to a limited number of individuals from among bankers, financiers, as well as to some initiated heads of state. Nowadays this notion has become apparent to the general public. With the advent of bitcoins this idea is now self-evident.

The definition of "play", proposed by Huizinga, is perhaps the only one that fits "money" with no reservations. Let us verify this:

1. Access to play is free, it is in fact a manifestation of freedom.
2. Play is distinct from "ordinary" or "real" life.
3. Play is distinct from "ordinary" life both as to locality and duration. "It contains its own course and meaning".
4. Play creates a certain order, it is order. Play requires an absolute and peculiar order.
5. Play is in no way connected with any material interest, and no profit can be gained by it.

Don't let that last point confuse you, indeed, a dollar can be put into business and gain profit, but it's a different game. Dollar is a convention accepted by you and by other players, and in this sense isn't any better than birch leaves that children pay with when playing supermarket.

Huizenga's work served as a starting point for the new economy of the twentieth century. It inspired John Nash, the Nobel Prize-winning mathematician, and subject of the blockbuster film 'A Beautiful Mind', to write his thesis on game theory in 1949, that featured the "Nash equilibrium", which caused a shift in the way we conceive market economy.

Basing our arguments on this first answer, let's analyze two more familiar events of the 20-th century that bear relevance on payment systems: the Great Depression and the dot-com bubble. Can you explain the reason for these crises in a few words? Don't you find it strange that such an explanation is impossible? Nevertheless, let's examine the background of these events.

In the early twentieth century, the United States was a developing country that did not have an evolved banking system of its own. The Bank of America was founded only in 1904 and at that time it was called – guess what – Bank of Italia. The situation evolved as follows: at that time there was already a lot of money in the United States, but no adequate means for its circulation yet. It's as if the mass of blood in the economic body was enormous, but its heart was as small as a child's fist, and its blood vessels were as thin as hair. During the First World War, the American economy had attracted enormous funds in military orders for Europe. A significant part of these proceeds were in the form of UK debt obligations. Meanwhile, the United States were forced to use the banking system of England. Having accumulated this wealth, the US attempted to enter the international financial market, which led to a full-scale banking war between Britain and the United States with a disastrous outcome for the US.

In 1928, Britain stepped out of the game by refusing to pay off military loans, and was soon followed by other European countries. It took a very short time for everyone to realize that the entire world economy is a game of trust. As soon as confidence started to fall apart it turned out that the US had swiftly lost 10 billion dollars of its budget. With the Great Depression (1929-1939) on his mind, Huizinga had written his book in 1938.

However, this is a rather remote history. Let's take a look at an important event of the recent past: the dot-com bubble burst. Here again we're looking at a crisis of trust breaking out when major players threw up the game. What was the context of this crisis? As we can see from the chronology of the crisis, the dot-com bubble had been swelling from 1993 to 2001. This is rather strange, because at the time the World Wide Web had only recently been invented by CERN nuclear scientists in 1994 and would take at least ten years to evolve into a thriving industry. By analogy, it took radio 75 years to attract 50 million users, and it took TV 15 years to boast a similar number of viewers. Yet, the Internet crossed, or should i say, jumped over this milestone in less than three years.

One way to explain this phenomenon would be to use complex economic theories. But in fact this was the work of one person: the US Vice President, Albert Gore. In his position as vice-president of the United States in the period from 1993 to 2001 he single-handedly created the Internet the way we know it. While he was still a senator, Gore pushed through a legislative initiative called the High Performance Computing Act of 1991. Within the framework of this initiative, he hammered out from the budget, which was pretty tight at the time, three billion dollars for the purpose of "speeding up the search for most effective ways of transforming the Internet into a commercially attractive business tool".

During the period of Gore's tenure as US Vice President, billions and billions of dollars in investments flowed into the Internet (on the average about $100 billion, according to experts), which brought about the inflation of the dot-com bubble. Amazon, eBay, Yahoo, all of these companies gained huge profits not from sales but directly from state budget for just being there in the "Internet business". Netscape browser, which AOL bought in

1998 for $4 billion, serves as a good illustration of this sort of "market value".

Quite predictably, as soon as it became clear that Gore is not going to win the presidential race and would step off the highest echelons of power, all financing was scaled back, and practically overnight it became apparent that an industry worth $1.7 trillion was not worth anything at all, while the flagship of the industry, Netscape, was in fact a throwaway application produced by a couple of students. The dot-com bubble burst with such a bang that it caused a massive recession in the US with GDP growth falling from 8% to 0%. This is how Internet was created from scratch to become a billion-dollar industry in just 3 years, and the economic mess was left for the Bush administration to take care of. In other words, Gore deliberately tapped into the experience of the Great Depression to perform a sort of "gravitational maneuver" to secure the US a head start of 10 years in technology ahead of the rest of the world.

As you can see, trust lies is at the very foundation of payment systems. Having made this clear, we can finally move on to consider the mechanisms underlying these systems.

Acknowledgments

I express my greatest gratitude to all those who helped me to work on this book:

To my wife **Gera Artimovich** for constant support. It was she who inspired me to publish my own textbook after leaving ChronoPay, where my ideas have not been heeded;

To my father, **Alexander Vladimirovich Artimovich**, for his understanding and faith in me;

To **Konstantin Popov** for painstaking correction of errors and improving on the textbook. His persistence contributed to the emergence of a logically related structure from scattered fragments of text;

To **Sergei Kalenik** for help in writing the introduction and publishing the textbook;

To **Svetlio Todorov** for invaluable guidance.

To **Shohdy Surur** for translation, editing and research of the European financial legislation.

Introduction

This book was conceived as a textbook for professionals working in the field of internet-acquiring and online payments, as well as for general public interested in the topic of electronic payments.

It is not my intention to gain profit from its publication, I just want to sum up many years of experience in the field.

I sincerely hope that my effort will help readers to enrich their knowledge in this field.

Each part of this book is logically divided into a number of chapters.

The structure of the book:

- Background
- Settlement participants
- Legislation
- The Rules of Payment Systems
- Technical integration
- Risks
- The cost of conducting Internet payments

Each chapter is supplemented with questions for self-control.

In Part One, we will be reviewing the development of the payment industry as a whole, particularly focusing on the United States, where it all had begun.

In Part Two, we will discuss the financial foundations, inquiring into the concepts of "bank", "bank account" and "bank-to-bank transfer".

In Part Three, we will cover Visa and Mastercard payment systems in detail. Part Four will be dealing with the high-risk category.

PART ONE

1. Background

The acceptance of credit cards by the general public gave rise to many related crimes that developed over the years. Criminals would deal in lost, stolen, and counterfeit cards as well as those obtained through submission of fraudulent credit card applications. Each of these crimes touched on identity theft although that term was not commonly used until many years later. If it were not for credit cards, I am convinced we would not have the extensive identity theft problem we have today. The simplicity of the crime in the early days and the abundance of readily available personal information set the stage for its staggering growth and impact. For that reason, it is fitting and necessary to know the history of credit cards and how they have become an indispensable part of our everyday existence.

Although the use of credit cards became commonplace in the 1970s, credit cards in various forms had been around for most of the twentieth century. In 1914. Western Union Telegraph Company offered its best customers a metal charge card that required a settlement of outstanding charges each month. It was the first consumer credit card and included deferred payments. These dogtag-style metal plates became commonplace and were later used by other retailers for their credit cards. They were embossed with the customer's name and address.

In 1924. a chain of California gas stations issued the first cardboard credit cards, setting the stage for the widespread use of oil and gas credit cards. This was an important development. The popularity of the automobile whetted the American public's appetite for travel and stoked the desire to be able to pay for gas anywhere. In the 1930s. department stores began to offer credit cards to their customers, and most used the metal plate style cards. Major department stores, including Bloomingdales. the now-defunct Gimbel's chain, and others, found that these cards were a customer draw as more and more people wanted them. By the 1940s. trendy restaurants and nightclubs offered their own credit cards that could be used only at the particular business establishment.

In 1948. the first bank credit card was introduced through a bank in Brooklyn. New York. It was called Charg-It and had similar payment terms to today's credit cards. Only local purchases could be made, and the cardholder had to have a bank account at that bank through which payments were made. The first bankcard, the Charg-it would not be the last and would open the door for other such cards and changes that would make them far more customer friendly.

In 1950. a visionary named Frank MacNamara conceived of a universal credit card that could be used at restaurants throughout New York City. The beauty of his idea was that instead of receiving monthly statements from each restaurant, as had been the norm, the cardholder would receive one statement each month for all restaurant activity. Thus was born the Diners Club credit card. The Diners Club card grew in popularity over the years and became the standard that others would emulate.

Long Island, New York banker Arthur Roth saw the future of credit and wanted to be in on it. His Franklin National Bank established a bank credit card for its customers in 1951. The card was a revolving credit card and could be used at stores and restaurants in the Long Island area. The card had no fees or interest but the balance had to be paid monthly. The bank made its money from the transaction fees paid by merchants accepting the cards. Franklin National Bank would eventually become European-American Bank (EAB), a powerhouse in banking. Citigroup would eventually purchase FAB. Many other banks also started issuing their own credit cards around this time.

In 1958. American Express got into the credit card business and its card quickly grew in popularity. The Hilton Hotel chain then came out with its own Carte Blanche credit card to compete with Diners Club and American Express. Although the big three credit card companies competed with each other, fraud had not yet emerged as a major problem. There were isolated stories of people without adequate income receiving cards and then going on huge spending sprees, unable to pay the subsequent statements. Yet the business model foretold future problems. The original model had been to extend credit to only the most worthy of customers, but the need to continually add new customers was critical to success. The result was that not all recipients of cards were as creditworthy as others.

In his excellent book on the history and evolution of credit cards entitled The Credit Card Catastrophe, author Matty Simmons asked, "In the rush to get more members, would cards be given to people only with dreams and no real way of paying lor those dreams?" We would sec many more examples of this in the years to come as the marketing arm of credit card issuers sometimes won out over the security department concerns.

Bank of America, a venerable financial institution, also wanted to be part of the credit card action. In 1958, it launched its BankAmericard and offered a revolving credit account. It started a campaign of sending unsolicited credit cards to people in California to grow its customer base. At the time, banks could do business only in the state where they had their charter. In order to reach the huge numbers of potential cardholders nationwide, BankAmericard worked out an ingenious interchange agreement with banks throughout the country. This agreement came to fruition in 1966, and the use of credit cards grew as millions more signed up. BankAmericard would eventually become the Visa card in 1976.

Also in 1966, another group of banks created a bank cooperative and named it the Interbank Card Association, to compete with BankAmericard. In 1969, this group purchased the rights to use the name Master Charge from the California Bank Association. The Interbank Card Association (1CA) was an umbrella organization for Master Charge and "governed by consensus among its member banks." It managed the various functions related to credit card administration including payments, authorizations, and settlement of charges for the association members. In 1979, Master Charge would be renamed MasterCard. The competition in the late 1960s resulted in large mailings of unsolicited credit cards. People received cards even though they may have not have been creditworthy or able to pay the charges. Children, the deceased, and family pets also got credit cards.

Large numbers of cards were stolen from the mail by Postal Service employees and others, resulting in an increasing amount of fraud losses to the industry'. Criticism of the practice of mailing unsolicited cards was extensive, even reaching the mainstream in a widely read 1970 Life magazine article. As Life observed: "American banks have mailed 100 million cards to unsuspecting citizens and have offered each recipient not only a handful of 'instant cash' but a dreamy method of buying by signature after the lettuce runs out." By this time, more than 1,400 banks offered its customers either Bank-Amcricard or Master Charge cards.

Congress reacted as expected and in 1970 passed a law forbidding the mailing of unsolicited cards. It enacted the Fair Credit Reporting Act and later the Fair Credit Billing Act in 1974 that amended 1968's Truth in Lending Act. But the stage was already set. Americans were becoming addicted to credit and their credit cards. And the threat of fraud and identity theft was only beginning.

At the end of the 2000s, Bitcoin emerged, a decentralized peer-to-peer electronic medium of exchange, that uses cryptography to control the creation and management of digital assets and its own open source protocol. All information about transactions between system addresses is included in the transaction log or blockchain.

On 3 January 2009, the bitcoin network came into existence, with Satoshi Nakamoto mining the genesis block of bitcoin, which had a reward of 50 bitcoins. The world's first bitcoin transaction on 12 January 2009, when a programmer Hal Finney downloaded the bitcoin software and received 10 bitcoins from Satoshi Nakamoto. The first known sale of bitcoins in U.S. dollars took place on October 12, 2009, when a user known as NewLibertyStandard sent $5.02 via PayPal to Martti Malmi, and Malmi sent 5,050 BTC to New Liberty Standard, enabling the site to establish the first-ever bitcoin trading service. NewLibertyStandart suggested to derive rate of BTC from the cost of electricity used by a computer to generate, or "mine" the currency.

The value of the first bitcoin transactions were negotiated by individuals on the bitcointalk forums with one notable transaction of 10,000 BTC used to indirectly purchase two pizzas delivered by Papa John's in May 2010.

Sure enough, Bitcoin, as well as other cryptocurrencies based on blockchain technologies, can in essence be used for reciprocal payments, in my opinion, there are some issues that have to be resolved before they may be designated as payment systems in their own right. These problems are most likely to be solved in near future, and cryptosystems will then become a very significant factor in the market of electronic payments.

There are quite a few payment systems around the world, such as PayPal, China UnionPay, JCB, etc., however, from my point of view, only Visa deserves to be called revolutionary.

Visa was the first to create such a structure, which is owned by all member banks, and by no bank in particular, emphasizing consensual decisions by all of its members. The creator of Visa, Dee Hock, coined a phrase for such a system of organization that blends characteristics of chaos and order, chaordic organization. Curiously enough, it was this particular feature that secured success and popularity of the system all over the world.

Bitcoin and subsequent cryptocurrencies that tap on the ideas of blockchain technology are similarly decentralized (with certain reservations). Furthermore, as a rule, they use tokens as accounting units that fall outside of the control of central banks and other government entities, unlike traditional payment systems that operate with fiat currencies issued by a recognizer authority or supported by a national credit system. That's both a catch and a fumble.

This book is about Visa and MasterCard payment systems.

2. Participants in card payment systems

With the proliferation of bank cards, checkbooks became a thing of the past. The advance of computer technologies has made it possible to conduct payments in a blink of an eye. For card payment networks to operate there is a need for a certain infrastructure that unites all of its participants. Such an infrastructure includes both the technical fit-out of participants, and the standards and rules that govern their interaction.

A universal card payment system may consist of the following parties:

- An issuing bank, also known as issuer, is a bank or financial institution that offers payment cards to consumers on behalf of the card networks.
- A cardholder is an individual to whom a card is issued on the basis of an agreement with the issuing bank.
- A company with financial license approved by Financial Conduct Authority (FCA) that regulates and supervises the conduct of more than 50,000 firms in the UK that provide financial products and services to both UK and international customers. The Prudential Regulation Authority (PRA) is responsible for the 'prudential regulation' and supervision of banks, building societies, credit unions, insurers and major investment firms. The FCA also regulates the prudential standards of firms not covered by the PRA.
- An acquirer, or acquiring financial institution, is a bank that processes credit or debit card transactions for businesses. Acquiring is processing and settling merchant's daily credit card transactions, and then in turn settling those transactions with the card issuer/association, as well as managing cash withdrawals by cardholders who are not clients of this banking institution. In this way, such a financial institution acquires, or serves as the intermediary, to facilitate the credit transaction and pays the merchant, less a discount fee for the service.
- Merchant trade organizations that accept cards payments for the goods and services provided on the basis of the

agreements signed with an acquirer. An individual entrepreneur can also act as a merchant providing goods and services. Another definition for such an enterprise is Point of Sale (POS).
- Settlement bank is a financial institution that performs settlements for transactions involving payment cards.
- Payment Service Provider (PSP) or Payment Processor is a legal entity or its structural subdivision that partners with Acquiring Banks to offer Merchants the informational and technical capability to accept payments. Payment Processor's activity is called processing and includes collection, processing and distribution of information on transactions with bank cards to settlement participants (settlement agents, issuers and acquirers).

A rather large number of PSPs became available with the development of the Internet. Until recently, a different term was widespread: Internet Payment Service Provider (IPSP). PSP normally allows retail outlets to accept cards from different payment systems, as well as to accept electronic money and other payment options. Normally PSP is connected to several acquiring banks. PSP simplifies the registration process for customers by assuming a significant part of the paper-work and technical processing, as well as technical integration with banks and providing customers with an integrated connection interface.

3. Legislation

Early on in the United States, credit cards (emphasis on *credit*) were distributed by regular mail, i.e. sent in envelopes to people's mailboxes. Eager to distribute of as many credit cards as possible, banks used phone books to collect addresses, which sometimes produced absurd situations with young children or even pets receiving a credit card. Credit cards theft from mailboxes became a common occurrence, and would often take place at the post office. As a result, banks suffered serious losses.

In 1970 US Congress finally passed a law forbidding the mailing of unsolicited cards. Statistics showed that most cases of credit card fraud during this period had to do with cards theft from purses and pockets.

A new statute to fight credit card fraud was created: **Title 15. United Slate Code. Section 1644, Fraudulent Use of Credit Cards**, was enacted in 1970. This statute was used to prosecute defendants for the "use of any counterfeit, fictitious, altered, forged, lost, stolen, or fraudulently obtained credit cards. However, this measure was not enough to reduce the number of fraudulent transactions with credit cards.

Finally, Congress enacted the Fair Credit Reporting Act and later the **Fair Credit Billing Act** in 1974 that amended 1968's Truth in Lending Act, which regulated the following nuances:

- Cardholders were given a 60-day period to dispute payment statement errors.
- Upon discovering an error, a cardholder has the option to protest a transaction by sending a letter to the issuing bank.
- A cardholder is not liable for unauthorized use of lost or stolen cards. It is sufficient to call the bank informing them of the incident. Despite the fact that the law sets a minimum amount for a transaction to $50 when using a card Face-to-Face, i.e. in presence of the holder, Visa and MasterCard do not apply this restriction. In case of fraudulent use of a card online or by phone, a cardholder is totally relieved of any liability.

The Fair Credit Billing Act is regarded as forerunner of chargeback.[1] Subsequently, this law was transformed into the rules of the International Payment Systems (IPS), which eventually expanded to include numerous amendments. The legislators acted wisely by ruling that since banks profited from each transaction and credit activities, they themselves should bear liability for the imperfections of the system the had established.

Visa USA website proclaims **Visa's Zero Liability**: "You are not liable for Unauthorized Use of your Card. You are protected if your card is lost, stolen or fraudulently used, online or offline."

In Russia, the massive emission of bank cards began in the 90s. The initial concerns regarding plastic cards were plentiful, since at the time financial institutions were busy trading in securities, and then a banking crisis broke out. For these reasons, no one earnestly engaged in the promotion of cards as a "safe method of payment".

On June 27, 2011, Law No. 161-FZ " **On the National Payment System** " came into force, which in 11-th paragraph of Article 9, " **Procedure for the use of electronic means of payment** ", gave the client one day to notify the issuing bank of a fraudulent transaction. Such a short time span to dispute a charge is incommensurable with US and EU regulations, which extend that period to 60 days and 8 weeks respectively.

In his book " **One from Many: VISA and the Rise of Chaordic Organization** " Dee Hawk regrets that he could not include merchants and cardholders as owner/members of the Visa organization putting them on a par with banks.

4. The Rules of Payment Systems

The **International Money Laundering Abatement and Financial Anti-Terrorism Act of 2001**, otherwise known as the **USA Patriot Act**, had a great impact on the world's financial system, which left its imprint on the rules of Visa and MasterCard payment systems.

In particular, the acquiring banks are now required to identify each trading point and its beneficial owners (this procedure is called Know Your Customer or KYC).

MasterCard introduced the concept of Transaction Laundering, i.e. situations when one merchant accepts money for the benefit of another, which allows an apparently legal merchant providing a cover-up for dozens of illegal ones trading in counterfeit medicines, for example.

Both payment systems prohibit such aggregation in its pure form and introduce the concept of Payment Faciliator to simplify processing for small and medium-sized stores. According to the rules, a Payment Faciliator is vested with rights to accept payments on behalf of its merchants. At the same time, the Faciliator takes on the task of performing most of the identification and settlement procedures, and also assumes all the risks for its clients.

Both payment systems are also using the *Merchant Location* rule, according to which the acquirer (just as payment facilitator) can enter into agreements with companies in the jurisdiction of its license (usually the aquirer's country) in order to accept funds.

For example, in Russia, all acquiring banks are licensed to connect merchants only from Russia. In the European Union, an acquirer can provide service to merchants from other EU member states.

5. Technical interaction and transaction security

5.1. Key events in the history of PCI DSS

Between 1988 and 1998, Visa and MasterCard report credit card fraud losses totaling 750 million dollars, a miniscule amount compared with hundreds of billions of dollars In transactions processed annually. Yet the Internet era Is about to change all that. As more merchants roll out e-commerce websites and connect their payment-processing systems to the Internet amid growing consumer comfort with online purchasing, fraudsters begin capitalizing on poorly protected systems to steal payment data, making payment card fraud faster and easier than ever before.

In October 1999, Visa approves Cardholder Information Security Program (CISP). Visa becomes the first card brand to develop security standards for merchants conducting online transactions. CISP is the first of several precursors to the PCI DSS.

In 2000, CyberSource reports that online revenue lost due to fraud has reached $1.5 billion; it would nearly triple throughout the course of the decade. By 2001, Visa reports that online credit card fraud rates were up to four times greater than the average transaction.

May 2001 was marked by a new event: Visa, other card brands struggle to enforce security policies. It turned out that only few companies are able to fully meet Visa's May 1, 2001, CISP compliance deadline because of disparities between Visa's North American and international guidelines. Similar security guidelines from the other card brands are less successful, largely because of the lack of a single, unified standard among the brands.

In July 2004, Web infrastructure attacks become rampant. Attacks against IIS[2] and other Web Infrastructure software components riddled with flaws highlight a technique becoming all too common. Attackers find and exploit vulnerable machines, plant keystroke loggers[3] and Trojans on them, and use that malware to steal payment card data. December 15, 2004, a hallmark day in the history of information security and compliance: the first unified security standard supported by all five major card brands, Payment Card Industry Data Security Standard (PCI DSS) 1.0, is released. Compliance with the standard has become mandatory for outlets and other organizations involved in the payment-processing cycle.

June 2005. All merchants processing at least 20,000 payment card transactions annually must be PCI DSS-compliant. While an increasing number of merchants allocate IT spending specifically toward security controls in support of PCI DSS compliance; many fall to be fully compliant by the deadline.

September 6, 2006. PCI DSS Version 1.1 released. The most notable addition to the first update to PCI DSS is Requirement 6.6, mandating that all custom application code must be professionally reviewed for vulnerabilities or a Web application firewall must be installed in front of Web-facing applications. In other words, before a data packet enters an application, it must pass through a firewall, where it is examined and, if found threatening, is rejected. In addition, the five major card brands (Visa, MasterCard, American Express, JCB and Discover) announce the creation of the PCI Security Standards Council (PCI SSC). an independent group that will manage the standard going forward.

Early 2008. The PCI SSC debuts the Payment Application Data Security Standard (PA-DSS). Based on best practices from Visa, the new sister standard to the PCI DSS is designed to help software vendors and others develop secure payment applications that do not store prohibited data, such as full magnetic stripe, CVV2 and PIN data.

October 1, 2008. PCI DSS version 1.2 released. Highlights of the updated guidance include new requirements regarding 802.1x for wireless network protection and antivirus for all operating systems. October 2010. PCI DSS 2.0 debuts. November 2013. PCI DSS 3.0 debuts.

August 2012. Compliance hits record levels. Visa reports that PCI DSS compliance among Level 1 merchants[4] reaches 97%, a record high. It is a clear sign that the industry's biggest merchants have made great strides to increase payment card data security.

5.2. Technical integration

Connecting an online store or an acquiring bank to a PSP payment gateway involves two types of integration:

1. Accepting and processing payment card data takes place at a payment gateway. The key point is that card data does not pass through the merchant's server, but goes directly to the payment gateway. Such an arrangement demands minimal actions on the part of merchant's technical staff in order to integrate the processing pages into online store. The entire responsibility for the safety of processing and storing card data, as well as its integrity when effecting payment, lies entirely with the payment gateway.
2. A merchant accepts card data through its own payment page, processes it independently (and, most likely, stores it in some form), then sends the data required for a transaction to a payment gateway through an Application Programming Interface (API) provided by Payment Processor. Such an arrangement demands a significantly higher level of technical competence from a merchant than in the first case. In this case a merchant carries more risks and, as a rule, must conform to the requirements of the PCI DSS standard. This issue is specially discussed in the corresponding chapter.

Most of the online stores opt for the first option, leaving the burden of card data processing on the payment gateways, which annually undergo PCI DSS audit.

The choice of the second option, which is more complex, expensive and associated with greater risk, may be justified for large companies. Such companies are need to run significant post-payment processing of the data received, such as doing statistical studies and data analysis to support making business decisions, etc. A company then needs to have the data at its disposal (otherwise, it would have to turn to Payment Processor for each sample of data), which justifies the transfer of data through merchant's servers.

6. The risks of Visa & MasterCard payment systems

What are the risks for users and members of Visa and MasterCard payment systems? Such risks can be logically divided into three subgroups: the risks for cardholders, for acquiring banks and for merchants. I intentionally set out a separate group for cardholders, because they are looked over all too often.

6.1. Potential risks for cardholders

The main risk for cardholders is that they can loose their money due to an attack. This can be done by intercepting the transmission of card data, since many of the online stores adopt transaction methods that allow the issuing bank to debit the client's account without his participation. At this point you may probably wonder why is this possible in the presence of 3-D Secure mechanism specifically designed to handle such situations by sending the buyer an SMS with one-time password for confirmation. However, 3-D Secure system was primarily developed for the benefit of acquiring banks in order to protect them from friendly fraud, although it is often promoted to cardholders as useful and meant for their protection. We will get back to this issue further on.

6.2. Potential risks for acquiring banks

An acquiring bank is fully responsible for its sales outlets within payment systems. Any fines imposed by the Association (e.g. for the sale of illegal merchandise) are debited from the acquiring bank, and not from the online store it contracted. In its turn, the bank will make every effort to pin it directly on the merchant, provided it still exists, and there are funds on its accounts.

However, the payment system settles its accounts with participants only on the third day. For in effect, the acquiring banks are providing loans to the merchants. In this way, chargeback are debited from the acquiring banks in the first instance. Such are the cases of not providing a service, or a transaction being taking place without cardholder's password confirmation (3-D Secure).

As mentioned above, 3-D Secure technology is designed to protect acquiring banks (and retail outlets) from friendly fraud in situations when cardholders themselves would protest their own transactions. Since the legislators shifted the responsibility for fraud onto the card issuing banks, while the payment systems eventually forwarded it to the acquiring banks, the problem of friendly fraud has become quite pressing.

A following situation may arise: a merchant sold goods to a buyer, a buyer paid with a card, then the next day the issuing bank goes bankrupt. Payment systems compensate for such risks by creating insurance funds, to with each participant contributes a certain sum.

It should be made clear here that some of the rules that have to do with deposits for members of Visa and MasterCard are closed for general public.

6.3. Potential risks for merchants

Merchants are exposed to the risk of non-reimbursement. Insurance funds of the payment system compensate for this risk, and the outcome for the merchant depends on whether the bank or the Payment Facilitator it had contracted will choose to play fair. It's worth noting, that the magnitude of the risks is directly proportional to the number of intermediaries in the money transfer chain. With more intermediaries risks get higher.

It should be noted here that in this context the Association is usually not an intermediary, as it is not directly involved in the transfer of funds from buyer to seller, but serves merely as an information gateway ensuring the transmission of data relating to funds flows between payer, acquirer and merchant. Simply put, at no moment in time do the funds moving from buyer to seller appear on the Association's settlement accounts. The

Association's task in general is to inform the acquiring bank of the buyer's card data, obtain from it a confirmation of a successful write-off of funds, and then inform the merchant that the payment has been made and it is now possible to deliver goods or provide services to the buyer, and finally inform the buyer that the payment has been made and he can now expect the merchant to provide the goods or services.

Merchant's risks are also due to the fact that, as a rule, the acquiring bank delegates to it the fines of the Association for violations of the rules of payment systems and for exceeding the number of chargebacks.

7. The cost of Conducting Internet payments

The costs of operations is directly determined by the payment system. It is composed of various factors. Early on in the development of the card industry, Visa and MasterCard had chosen a strategy that allowed both the issuer and the bank to profit from issuing cards and effecting payments, respectively. This strategy proved to be a 100% valid. Issuer's allowances for each transaction contributed to an increase in emission of cards, while acquirer's allowances helped the growth of acquiring.

These two components determine the cost of payments through Visa and MasterCard. At the same time, contributions to the issuing bank usually exceed by manifold the commission earned by the acquiring bank. The issuing bank's fees are called Interchange Fees (IF). In the US, Visa and MasterCard disclosed their information on the amount of interchange fees in 2006 after a prolonged conflict with merchants.

All over the world, the card payment systems and merchants are engaged in constant feuds. The latter deeply resent the excessively high rates of IF. Banks justify their position by high infrastructure maintenance costs of support services, offices, and ATMs. I never attempted calculating the actual cost of cards servicing, however, it is my firm conviction that a reduction of IF costs would solely benefit merchants, but not the rest of participants in a payment system. It is evident though, that with IF reduction, the ultimate price of goods for the buyer would not change. However, this would lower the product cost, which includes the cost of IF, and its reduction would benefit merchants by raising their profits. Whereas, the card issuing bank will come off a loser, which will reduce its motivation to issue new cards. In other words, the attempts to reduce IF will inevitably lead to serious setbacks in the card payments market.

In 2016, after a month of negotiations on the issue of IF reduction with Visa, the Wallmart's refused to accept Visa cards in a number of its Canadian stores for a period for 6 months. According to data provided by Wallmart, its annual expenses for Interchange amounted to $100 million. This largest global retail giant and Visa finally came to a mutual agreement in early 2017.

List of sources used

- Martin T. Biegelman – Identity Theft Handbook: Detection, Prevention, and Security.
- https://searchsecurity.techtarget.com/feature/The-history-of-the-PCI-DSS-standard-A-visual-timeline

Self-control questions

1. What was the purpose of Fair Credit Billing Act?
2. Name the participants in card payment systems.
3. What is PCI SSC?
4. What are the main steps for technical integration with a PSP payment gateway?
5. Name the potential risks of Visa & MasterCard payment systems for participants.
6. What are Interchange Fees?

PART TWO

Financial system basics

In order to understand the process of mutual settlements within any payment system, it is important to know the principles of the money flow between banks, as well as to understand what do financial institutions stand for and what laws regulate their activities.

1. Legal Principles

The European Union constitutes an internal market defined by the "four freedoms": the free movement of capital, people, goods and services – including financial services. The euro area comprises those EU member states that have adopted the euro as their currency. The euro area is a monetary union with a single currency, a common central bank system (the Eurosystem), a single monetary policy and a common money market.

Most of the payment, clearing and settlement infrastructures in the euro area and the broader EU were originally created with the aim of meeting the needs of individual countries. They were rather diverse in nature and not necessarily suited to the needs of an internal market, let alone the needs of a single currency area. Financial integration, globalisation have led to an overhaul and reshaping of the infrastructure for effecting payments and for the trading, clearing and settlement of financial instruments. The introduction of the euro in 1999 has furthered efforts to harmonise or consolidate infrastructure. The Eurosystem comprises the European Central Bank (ECB) and the national central banks (NCBs) of all the countries in the euro area.

The system of payment and settlement in EU is governed by a complex of legal norms that broadly fall into the following categories:

- international standards;
- provisions of national law;
- provisions of public law.

International standards are set in EU directives and other regulatory documents governing cross-border settlement relations that deal with:

- coordination of banking laws;
- services for the management of payment transactions;
- protection of interests of participants of payment systems;
- functional characteristics of mutual settlements and safety of settlement funds;
- legal security for the participants of payment systems and customers;
- European standards for foreign transfers;
- legal norms for final settlements within payment systems;
- facilitation of overseas transfers;
- improving the transparency of payment transactions for customers;
- equal treatment for foreign and domestic transactions;
- general provision for the circulation of euro;
- rules for settlement of securities;
- international agreements governing the rules for circulation of bill and check.

The provisions of private laws reflect the national norms that define general civil legal relations and include such legislation as:

- civil Code;
- credit transfer acts;
- commercial Code;
- laws governing the circulation of checks and bills;
- general rules of economic activity.

In addition, private law also refers to clearing and settlement system regulation, as well as general and special rules for conducting business activities.

Public law provisions are generally comprised of:

1. regulations of the national central bank or other body supervising the banking and financial activities in the country;
2. regulations governing credit institutions, banking operations, financial services and transactions;
3. laws preventing money laundering;
4. various tax and payment regulations.

The norms and laws of private and public law may vary for the EU member-countries and hence special normative acts are being developed for their coordination.

The European Union Treaty defines the main objectives of the European System of Central Banks (ESCB) as that of facilitating the smooth functioning of the payment system across the European Union. The Statutes of the European System of Central Banks (ESCB) and the European Central Bank state that the ECB has the right to issue decrees ensuring the efficiency and reliability of the settlement and payment systems within the European community as well as for transactions with third countries.

The ESCB Statute defines one of its principal tasks as that of ensuring a flawless operation of the payment transactions. The Governing Council of the ECB, which includes the governors of national central banks and members of the ECB Board of Directors, produced a uniform policy in the field of payment transactions, that makes no distinction between large-value settlement systems and retail payment systems.

2. Financial institutions

The European Central Bank (ECB) maintains lists of the following five groups of institutions, based on information provided regularly by all members of the European System of Central Banks (ESCB):

- Monetary financial institutions (MFIs)
- Investment funds (Ifs)

- Financial vehicle corporations (FVCs)
- Payment statistics relevant institutions (PSRIs)
- Insurance corporations (ICs)

Monetary financial institutions (MFIs) are resident credit institutions as defined in European Union (EU) law, and other resident financial institutions whose business is to receive deposits and/or close substitutes for deposits from entities other than MFIs and, for their own account (at least in economic terms), to grant credits and/or make investments in securities.

More precisely, Regulation ECB/2013/33 concerning the balance sheet of the monetary financial institutions sector defines MFIs as resident undertakings that belong to any of the following sectors:

- **central banks**, i.e. national central banks of the EU Member States and the European Central Bank;
- **credit institutions** as defined in Article 4(1)(1) of Regulation (EU) No 575/2013 of the European Parliament and of the Council of 26 June 2013 on prudential requirements for credit institutions and investment firms;
- **other deposit-taking corporations** which are principally engaged in financial intermediation and whose business is:
  - to receive deposits and/or close substitutes for deposits from institutional units, not only from MFIs, and
  - to grant loans and/or make investments in securities for their own account (at least in economic terms), or
  - electronic money institutions, as defined in Article 2(1) and (2) of Directive 2009/110/EC, that are principally engaged in financial intermediation in the form of issuing electronic money;
- **money market funds** (MMFs) , **i.e. collective investment undertakings as defined in Article 2 of Regulation ECB/2013/33.**

3. Non-banking Financial Institutions (NBFIs)

At a basic level, a non-bank financial institution provides some banking services without meeting the legal definitions of a bank, or financial Institutions operating without a license. This can cover many forms, as many types of institutions offer some financial services without qualifying as a bank. Among the many types of businesses that might serve as a non-bank finance company are: Insurance firms, Check-cashing services, Pawn shops, Hedge funds, Payday lenders, Currency exchanges.

Some non-banking finance companies may better serve customers who can't be served efficiently by banks, or those who banks do not seek as customers. For example, a check-cashing outlet can provide low-income customers a less expensive alternative than a bank, if the bank charges fees for those unable to maintain a minimum deposit.

NBFIs supplement banks in providing financial services to individuals and firms. They can provide competition for banks in the provision of these services. While banks may offer a set of financial services as a package deal, NBFIs unbundle these services, tailoring their services to particular groups. Additionally, individual NBFIs may specialize in a particular sector, gaining an informational advantage. By this unbundling, targeting, and specializing, NBFIs promote competition within the financial services industry.

Having a multi-faceted financial system, which includes non-bank financial institutions, can protect economies from financial shocks and recover from those shocks. NBFIs provide multiple alternatives to transform an economy's savings into capital investment, which act as backup facilities should the primary form of intermediation fail.

3.1. Distinctive features of the Russian NBFIs

- There is a narrow specialization for Non-banking Financial Organizations (abbreviated as NKO) within the Russian credit system – their sole purpose is to conduct settlements.
- Russian NKOs are not allowed to accept funds from legal

entities and individuals as deposits for the purpose of allocation on their own behalf and for their own account.
- NKOs are not allowed to engage in production, trade and insurance activities.

The NKO appeared on the Russian banking market for the first time in the early 1990s at the recommendation of the International Monetary Fund amidst a situation of bank non-payments and a system of surrogate settlements based on barter with the prospect of servicing new systems of settlements: interbank, stock exchange, corporate, etc.

4. Banks

Banks are financial intermediaries that take funds from depositors, pool that money and lend it to those seeking funds. They make money, in part, by paying depositors less interest than they charge borrowers and pocketing the difference. Banks often offer checking and savings accounts, certificates of deposit, personal and business loans, mortgages and credit cards.

The European System of Central Banks (ESCB) consists of the European Central Bank (ECB) and the national central banks (NCBs) of all 28 member states of the European Union (EU).

The ESCB is not the monetary authority of the eurozone, because not all EU member states have joined the euro. That role is performed by the Eurosystem, which includes the national central banks of the 19 member states that have adopted the euro. The ESCB's objective is price stability throughout the European Union. Secondarily, the ESCB's goal is to improve monetary and financial cooperation between the Eurosystem and member states outside the eurozone.

5. EU rules on payment services

The EU set up common rules for payments with the adoption of the first payment services directive (PSD 1) in 2007. The payment services directive established the same set of rules on payments across the whole European Economic Area (European Union, Iceland, Norway and Liechtenstein), covering all types of electronic and non-cash payments, such as

- credit transfers
- direct debits
- card payments
- mobile and online payments

The directive laid down rules about the information that payment services providers have to give to consumers and about the rights and obligations linked to the use of payment services. The directive introduced a new category of payment service providers other than banks – the so-called 'payment services'. This has increased competition and choice for consumers.

The directive also laid the groundwork for the Single Euro Payments Area (SEPA), which allows consumers and businesses to make payments under the same conditions across the euro area.

The **revised Payment Services Directive (PSD2)**, which applies as of 13 January 2018, aims to modernize Europe's payment services to the benefit of both consumers and businesses, so as to keep pace with this rapidly evolving market.

The new rules:

- Prohibit surcharging, which are additional charges for payments with consumer credit or debit cards, both in shops or online;
- Open the EU payment market to companies offering payment services, based on them gaining access to information about the payment account;
- Introduce strict security requirements for electronic payments and for the protection of consumers' financial data;
- Enhance consumers' rights in numerous areas. These include reducing the liability for non-authorized payments and introducing an unconditional ("no questions asked") refund right for direct debits in euro.

Consumers will be better protected against fraud and other abuses and payment incidents, with improved security measures in place. As regards losses that consumers may face, the new rules streamline and further harmonize the liability rules in case of unauthorized transactions, ensuring enhanced protection of the legitimate interests of payment users. Except in cases of fraud or gross negligence by the payer, the maximum amount a payer could, under any circumstances, be obliged to pay in the case of an unauthorized payment transaction will decrease from €150 to €50.

6. Consumer rights

PSD1 and PSD2 protect consumer rights in the event of unauthorized debits from an account under certain conditions. A direct debit is a payment that is not initiated by the payer, but by the payee on the basis of consent of the payer to the payee. It is based on the following concept: "I request money from someone else with their prior approval and credit it to myself". The payer and the biller must each hold an account with a payment service provider and the transfer of funds (money) takes place between the payer's bank and the biller's bank. However, since the biller can collect funds from a payer's account, provided that a mandate has been granted by the payer to the biller, the payer should also have a right to get the money refunded. Member States have applied different rules with regard to this issue.

Under PSD1, payers had the right to a refund from their payment service provider in case of a direct debit from their account, but only under certain conditions. In order to enhance consumer protection and promote legal certainty further, PSD2 provides a legislative basis for an unconditional refund right in case of a SEPA direct debit during an 8 week period from the date the funds are debited form the account. The right to a refund after the payee has initiated the payment still allows the payer to remain in control of his payment. In such cases, payers can request a refund even in the case of a disputed payment transaction.

7. Pan-European settlement and payment systems

At present, the pan-European settlement and payment system consists of the ECB's gross settlement system and several settlement systems that operate under the auspices of the Euro Banking Association (EBA).

The Euro Banking Association (EBA) was founded in Paris in

1985 by 18 commercial banks and the European Investment Bank. The European Commission as well as the Bank for International Settlements (BIS) supported the founding of the EBA. Since then, the number of members has risen to almost 200. The institutions come from all member states of the European Union as well as from Norway, Switzerland, Australia, China, Japan, the United Arab Emirates and the United States. In its early years, the agenda of the EBA included the promotion of the European Monetary Union (EMU) and the development and management of a private industry ECU clearing system stretching across Europe.

For the start of the EMU, the EBA delivered EURO1, a RTGS-equivalent large-value payment system for single eurotransactions. The EBA also developed STEP1, a payment service for single euro payments of high priority and urgency for small and medium-sized banks, and STEP2, a Pan-European Automated Clearing House (PE-ACH), which processes euro retail payments. All three payment systems are run by EBA Clearing.

Core Principles for Systemically Important Payment System serve as a technological basis for the operation of pan-European payment systems. EU laws and directives regulating the operation of payment systems are aimed at creating a unified system of legal relations in the EU area and implementing the principles of conducting settlements and payments set forth in the documents of the Bank for International Settlements.

TARGET2 (Trans-European Automated Real-time Gross settlement Express Transfer system, second generation) is the real-time gross settlement system (RTGS) for large-value and urgent payments in euros owned and operated by the Eurosystem. It plays a pivotal role in implementing the single monetary policy and in the functioning of the euro money market by offering a real-time settlement service in central bank money with broad market coverage. In the absence of any upper or lower value limit it has attracted a variety of other payments.

TARGET2 replaced the first-generation RTGS system for the euro. TARGET commenced operations on 4 January 1999, a few days after the launch of the euro. TARGET was built by linking together the different RTGS structures that already existed at national level as there was not sufficient time to develop a single system. However, this decentralized structure proved inefficient and costly in the long term.

TARGET2 came into being as a redesign of TARGET and offers harmonized core services on a single technical platform. Three Eurosystem central banks – the Bank of Italy, the Bank of France and the Deutsche Bundesbank (known as the 3CB) – jointly provide the SSP and operate it on behalf of the Eurosystem. The system is based on a single technical infrastructure, the Single Shared Platform (SSP). TARGET2 fully replaced the first-generation TARGET by May 2008. The move from a decentralized multi-platform system to a technically centralized platform made it possible for TARGET2 to offer harmonized technical and business services at EU level, ensuring a level playing field for banks across Europe, supported by a single price structure applicable to both domestic and cross-border transactions.

8. Single Euro Payments Area (SEPA)

The Single Euro Payments Area (SEPA) project was set up by the banking industry with a view to achieving a fully integrated market for retail payment services in the euro area, with no distinction between cross-border and national payments in euros. The first phase of the SEPA initiative was officially launched in January 2008, and as of 2018, SEPA consists of the 28 member states of the European Union

SEPA clearance is based on the IBAN bank-account identification. Domestic euro transactions are routed by IBAN; earlier national-designation schemes were abolished by February 2014, providing uniform access to the new payment instruments.

The different functionalities provided for by SEPA are divided into separate payment schemes, detailed below.

SEPA Credit Transfer (SCT) allows for the transfer of funds from one bank account to another. SEPA clearing rules require that payments made before the cutoff point on a working day, be credited to the recipients account within one working day.

SEPA Instant Credit Transfer (SCT Inst), also called SEPA Instant Payment, provides for instant crediting of a payees (less than ten seconds, initially, with a maximum of twenty seconds in exceptional circumstances).

This scheme was launched in November 2017, and was at that time operational for end customers in eight euro zone countries, and is expected soon to be available in most euro zone countries and potentially in all SEPA countries.

SEPA Direct Debit Direct debit functionality is provided by two separate schemes. The basic scheme, Core SDD, was launched on 2 November 2009, and is primarily targeted at consumers. Participation by banks offering SEPA payments is compulsory. In addition, there is a second scheme, B2B SDD, targeted towards business users. It requires a mandate be submitted to the bank by both the creditor and debtor. Among other differences, it does not allow the debtor to request a refund from its bank after its account has been debited. Participation in the scheme is optional.

An instant 24/7/365 payment scheme named SCT Inst went live on November 21, 2017 allowing instant payment 24 hours a day and 365 days a year. The participating banks will handle the user interface and security, like for existing SEPA payments, e.g. web sites and mobile apps.

9. BASE II Clearing System Basics

The BASE II Clearing System is the international electronic clearing system supporting transaction-based payment exchange between Visa members. Clearing is the process by which Visa collects data about a transaction from the source, validates the information and calculates fees, values the transaction (calculates the base value of the transaction, as well as various fees and charges), and then delivers it to the destination. The destination uses this information to post the transaction to the cardholder's account or reconcile a merchant's settlement position. BASE II Clearing is one of Visa's core processing functions, ensuring that merchants get paid and enabling members to manage the accounts of cardholders. From a business standpoint, the clearing system is complex due to the number of regions it covers, and the need to adapt the system to keep up with specialized arrangements by members, unique banking regulations, legal agreements, and changing political landscapes.

BASE II's strengths include:

- Brand-Agnostic Processing—It supports all cards (Visa, MasterCard, American Express, etc.) and several non-card payment services. BASE II will edit, assess fees, and create the necessary settlement information without considering what brand name the transaction occurred under. It also performs processing based on unique rule sets requested by members.
- Continuous Clearing and Settlement Processes—BASE II is a transaction engine that is continually running: collecting files, stripping out records, creating trail balances and settlement positions. At any one time, it has upwards of 200 collection files open and being processed.
- Extraordinary Power and Capacity—BASE II's role as a core processing component means it must run with 100 percent reliability while it processes an average of about 100 million transactions per day (2006 statistic). In addition to member-to-member interfaces, BASE II also supports exchange/transport of data for many other Visa services, in total managing an average of 1.5 billion records daily (2006 statistic).

10. VisaNet

The BASE II Clearing system collects and delivers Visa transaction data, often referred to as interchange, through the Visa transaction processing and communications network known as VisaNet.

VisaNet is the processing platform that connects Visa and its 21,000 worldwide member banks and financial institutions so that they can authorize and settle electronic payments quickly and securely. The VisaNet network is comprised of hardware and software, including BASE II, which perform transaction processing and are attached to communications facilities that connect with members' systems and other networks. The network has a low risk, redundant infrastructure (i.e., backup generators, duplicate equipment, multiple routes for a transaction to get to its destination, etc.) that eliminates single points of failure and enables it to be available 24 hours a day.

Depending on the region, VisaNet supports a wide variety of transactions, including: purchase; cash and bill payment transactions made with any card; cardholder transfer; recurring payment transactions; and ATM transactions for other networks such as Plus. These transactions are processed through VisaNet's authorization (VisaNet Integrated Payment system), clearing (BASE II), and settlement services. The flow of the services is as follows:

1. **Authorization** — The process by which an issuer approves or declines a cardholder's transaction before a purchase is finalized or cash is disbursed.
2. **Clearing** — The process by which Visa collects transaction data from the acquirer, values the transaction, enforces risk services, calculates fees and charges, and delivers the validated information to the issuer for posting to the cardholder's account.
3. **Settlement** — The process of accumulating advices from clearing, determining each members' net settlement position (in other words, who owes what to whom), and initiating the exchange of funds.

11. Who can issue banks card in Europe?

Historically, partnerships with Visa in Europe have taken the form of memberships. The following are the main types of membership:

Principal Member. A Principal Member can issue cards and acquire merchants directly. They can process transactions and provide processing services. A Principal Member is required to settle funds directly with Visa Europe. A Principal Member may also sponsor Associate Members or Participant Members.

Associate Member. An Associate Member must be sponsored for Visa Europe membership by a Principal Member. Associate Members may, subject to written agreement with their sponsoring Principal Member, undertake almost all Principal Member activities. The main difference between a Principal and Associate Member is that an Associate Member's card and sales volumes will be attributed to its sponsor as the sponsor will be liable for settlement with Visa Europe.

Participant Member. A Participant Member must be sponsored for membership of Visa Europe by a Principal Member or an Associate Member. Participant Members are not permitted to undertake issuing or acquiring activities. They assist their sponsoring member perform its Visa Europe activities and only perform such functions in agreement with and on behalf of the sponsoring Member.

12. SWIFT

The Society for Worldwide Interbank Financial Telecommunications (SWIFT) is an international interbank system providing a network that enables financial institutions worldwide to send and receive information about financial transactions in a secure, standardized and reliable environment. It's also known as SWIFT-BIC (Bank Identifier Codes), BIC code, SWIFT ID or SWIFT code. SWIFT was co-founded in 1973 by 239 banks from 15 countries. It provides fast, safe and reliable exchange of financial messages around the world.

SWIFT is a cooperative society under Belgian law owned by its member financial institutions (over 9,000 banks from 209 countries as for 2010). Its headquarters are in La Hulpe, near Brussels. AT present, SWIFT members are more than 10,000 organizations, including about 1000 corporations.

More than 1 million transactions on money transfers, interbank payments, securities are daily conducted through SWIFT. The annual number of payment orders that pass through SWIFT is over 2.5 billion.

Within the system each bank has its own unique SWIFT code. In practice, in order to make a payment in Europe it is enough to know the name and the IBAN code of the beneficiary's bank account that contains an interpreted SWIFT code.

After the events of September 11, 2001, the CIA and the US Treasury gained access to the financial information of SWIFT network in order to track possible financial transactions by terrorists.

Advantages:

- high speed of transfer. A SWIFT money transfer to anywhere in the world takes on average from 1-3 days to 1 minute;
- no restrictions on the amount of payment;
- reliable confidentiality preservation of information provided by a number of organizational and technical measures;
- a large selection of currencies for settlements within the system;
- substantially lower tariffs in comparison with other payment systems;
- the ability to transfer money to virtually anywhere in the world due to a widespread popularity of SWIFT;
- the sender is not obliged to have a bank account.

Disadvantages:

- the time it takes for a transfer to complete. Since payments are processed by different banks at different speed, there is always a risk that it will get "stuck" at one of them. The delays are due to sanctions applied to different jurisdictions and participating banks that conduct a transaction. Possibly this is the only negative aspect of SWIFT.

The model of SWIF is quite simple. As already mentioned, each member bank of the payment system is assigned its own unique SWIFT code, which serves as an identifier for transferring funds between banks within a country and abroad. The path from sending bank to recipient's bank is called a chain or route of payment. The chain consists from two to several banks around the globe. The settlement between them is carried out through correspondent accounts. SWIFT path is constructed as follows: the sending bank sends a SWIFT message to its correspondent, the correspondent sends a message to a correspondent bank geographically located as close as possible to a bank of the country where the recipient of funds is located. For example, consider a transfer from Russia to Argentina. The sending bank will try to send money to the correspondent bank in Argentina. If there no direct correspondent relations between these banks exist, the closest country where it is available will be chosen, for example, a bank in Brazil. The cycle will be repeated until the funds reach the recipient. There are also large correspondent banks (nodal points), which other banks address in the first instance when conducting SWIFT payments. Local legislation, in turn, can change the route of SWIFT transfer to pass through certain mandatory points. Other participants may also be present in the payment route.

List of sources used

- Regulatory process in financial services (ec.europa.eu)
- Payment systems in the euro area (bis.org/cpmi/paysys/ecbcomp.pdf)
- Payment Services Directive: frequently asked questions (ec.europa.eu)

Self-control questions

1. What types of financial institutions do you know?
2. What is a Non-banking Financial Institutions?
3. What is PSD2?
4. What is direct debit?
5. What is the regulation for consumer rights protection in the EU?
6. What is SEPA?
7. What is the role of VisaNet?
8. Describe VisaNet flow of the services.
9. What is SWIFT?
10. Describe the translation path in SWIFT system.

PART THREE

Visa and MasterCard

1. The Evolution of Payment Systems

1.1. The Evolution of Visa

The early version of this chapter was quite succinct. Eventually I decided to quote fragments of the book «One from Many: VISA and the Rise of Chaordic Organization» by VISA's founder, Dee Hock,6 in which he relates the story of creation of the largest financial structure in the world. The success of this man is stunning. He had accomplished the impossible task of rallying hundreds of banks around the world in one organization, and his story is worth reading. Every payment industry expert should be aware of his name and the history of Visa.

Quotes from the book are in italics. The history of VISA is divided into four parts, and the amount of information is quite large.

1.1.1. Part One

Today, before any audience in the world, I can hold a Visa card overhead and ask, "How many of you recognize this?" Every hand in the room will go up. When I ask, "How many of you can tell me who owns it, how it's governed, or where to buy shares?" a dead silence comes over the room. Something incredible happened, but what, and how?

(Dee Hock is the founder and former CEO of Visa)

As Dee Hock himself writes, it took him two years to create a new type organization, and another 14 years to get his brainchild into shape. After 16 years of dedicated service as Director General of Visa, Dee Hock left his job and the business world to spend almost a decade in relative seclusion, working on a 200-acre estate on the Pacific coast west of the Silicon Valley.

I am yanked back into the moment by a gust of wind laden with icy drops of rain. While we have wandered, the sky has darkened, the wind has picked up, and daylight has dimmed. No doubt of it, we're in for a heavy storm. Better hurry. Rain will soon saturate the soil and work will be impossible. A flick of the throttle and Thee Ancient One roars to life. We crawl across the land pushing a huge pile of brush toward the ravine. Unconsciously I slip out of harmony with my surroundings to take control of the situation. One hurried pass, then another and a third. Faster, faster—fifteen minutes more and the job will be done.

The Ancient One screams with metal on metal, bucks, and stops to the hammering of drive-wheel spokes jumping the track sprocket. Damn and double damn! Idiot! Fool! I would try to impose control and demand more than the situation required, or Thee could give. I shut down the engine and sit quietly in the rain as anger and frustration slowly drain away. I begin to grin. Plus one for Thee, ancient one. Minus one for you, old man.

Within three years, air and sunlight will transform the subsurface mudstone shattered by Thee Ancient One's rippers into clay. The clay will suck nitrogen from the roots of the grasses and mix with dying stems. Thousands of gophers, mice, and moles are at work, assiduously carrying grass underground and dirt to the surface.

Billions of worms, ants, beetles, and other creatures till the soil around the clock. Trillions of microscopic creatures live, eat, excrete, and die beneath my feet. In time, larger animals and birds will return to make their contribution. Porous soil will build to absorb and distribute water from even the heaviest storms, and lateral ditches that now control runoff can be filled. Each year grasses, flowers, shrubs, and trees will be taller, thicker, more diverse, and healthy.

The next fragment needs an additional remark to be properly understood. Dee Hock is known to be an ardent opponent of the modern hierarchical organizations (characterized by centralization of power and authoritarian management). Notably Hock's non-standard thinking was the cause of a series of dismissals from the companies he had worked for.

Nearly four decades ago, three questions emerged from the constant dialogue with Old Monkey Mind. They were fascinating then. They are compelling today. They had everything to do with the origins of Visa. Time and time again they return, always more demanding.

Why are organizations, everywhere, political, commercial, and social, increasingly unable to manage their affairs? Why are individuals, everywhere, increasingly in conflict with and alienated from the organizations of which they are part?

Why are society and the biosphere increasingly in disarray?

Today, it doesn't take much thought to realize we're in the midst of a global epidemic of institutional failure. Not just failure in the sense of collapse, such as might occur to a building or a business, but the more common and pernicious form: organizations increasingly unable to achieve the purpose for which they were created, yet continuing to expand as they devour resources, demean the human spirit, and destroy the environment.

Every system is in need of control, and big changes require a strong leader. However, a healthy natural system is defined by control being evenly distributed, and changes occurring continuously.

National Bank of Commerce

In 1965, Dee Hock finally settled in the National Bank of Commerce (NBC), one of Seattle's local banks, where he performed "temporary assignments," because at that time "there were no open positions commensurate with his experience" at the bank.

Bank of America (BofA) has decided to franchise BankAmericard credit cards. NBC became one of the six licensing banks of this program and was intending to be in business within ninety days. NBC President Maxwell Carlson appointed Bob Cummings to head the program and suggested that they "borrow" Dee Hock to assist him.

Within two weeks, Bob and Dee were in San Francisco for training at the Bank of America Service Corporation, a division of BofA, along with representatives of other licensee banks. It turned out that there was bad blood and limited communication between the BankAmericard center and the licensing corporation. They reported to different segments of the bank. Worse yet, the bank's own card center had no capacity to comply with rules prescribed in the licensing agreements. The National Bank of Commerce, had already made a public announcement of its BankAmericard program. It had a forty-year correspondent banking relationship with the Bank of America. Founders of both banks have been close friends. There was no way to reverse the decision NBC had made. Bob and Dee were in deep trouble.

There was no choice for Bob and Dee but to design a BankAmericard program for NBC out of their collective experience, knowledge of the market, and what they could glean from the diverse experience of others. Most of the Bank of America training material went into the trash.

To solve the problems, they ordered a thousand imprinters[5] at $35 each, two hundred thousand plastic cards and several expensive card embossers. The team commandeered the bank auditorium next to the cafeteria, then "borrowed" all willing, unassigned employees, and all those who could be spared for ninety days, no questions asked.

Ads went in the paper for credit analysts, merchant sales representatives, collectors, and other essential personnel not readily available in the bank. It wasn't quite send me "the wretched refuse of your teeming shores," but it was similar.

Within the month they were in the last of many grueling meetings across the state, in an effort to qualify 120,000 bank customers for credit cards. The results are spectacular. The people in each branch self-organize the work, and within the month, letters are on the way to 120,000 customers, offering them a card. Solving emerging problems as they arose the team created a credit card program almost from scratch by the end of 1966. One hundred thousand clients received the promised credit cards.

In the beginning, there was no magnetic strip on the card and no electronic card readers at point of sale. Cards were placed in the bed of a manual imprinter, a four-part sales draft placed on top and a lever pulled or pressed to create an impression. They were dubbed "zip zap" machines. Imprinters were purchased by banks for a few dollars and rented to merchants for handsome monthly fees. Many banks were incensed when imprinters they had supplied were used to serve cardholders of competitors.

A year after the launch of the effort at NBC, Dee Hock headed the credit card department.

Problems

Meanwhile, the merchant bank, having already been paid and under immense pressure to handle its own cardholder transactions, had no incentive to process foreign transactions and get them to the issuing bank for billing to the cardholder. Since each bank was both a merchant-signing bank and a card-issuing bank, they began to play tit-for-tat, while back rooms filled with unprocessed transactions, customers went unbilled, and suspense ledgers swelled like a hammered thumb. It became an accounting nightmare.

The system for clearing sales drafts between banks was primitive, cumbersome, and impossible to fully describe—nor is it necessary to the story to understand this brief summary. There were no electronic data entry or clearing systems. Each merchant - signing bank accepted all transactions regardless of the issuing bank, crediting the merchant account for the total, manually sorted the transactions by issuing bank, and reimbursed themselves by drawing a clearing draft on each issuing bank through the Federal Reserve System. When the clearing draft reached the issuing bank, it was posted to a suspense ledger while waiting for the merchant bank to keypunch the sales drafts and send them through the U. S. mail.

Criminals sensed a bonanza. Within months, large quantities of plastic cards not yet embossed with cardholder names and numbers began to disappear from manufacturers' warehouses, shipping companies, and bank storage facilities. A few thousand dollars for embossing machines, some organized pilferage of account numbers from discarded copies of sales drafts, and the crooks were in the counterfeit card business.

Counterfeit cards were soon more than matched by cards stolen wholesale on their way through postal departments, pilfered from mailboxes by thieves, snatched by pickpockets, and "forgotten" by customers, with assistance from conniving store clerks. Thousands of counterfeit and stolen cards were soon on the black market, selling for as little as $50, each card swiftly used to purchase and resell thousands *of dollars of merchandise before being abandoned.*

Sham merchants appeared, depositing large quantities of fraudulent sales drafts during the weeks it took banks to process them through the system, then vanishing with the money as complaints piled up.

There were no electronic data entry or clearing systems. Each merchant had a floor limit, beneath which no authorization was required. It took criminals no time at all to pattern such limits and accurately assess the degree of risk in each merchant location. A transaction over the floor limit required that a merchant employee telephone the bank with which they had contracted. An employee of the merchant bank then made a longdistance call to the card-issuing bank, where an employee manually looked up the customer's account in huge, computer-printed, paper ledgers, determined if the sale could be authorized, gave an authorization number to the inquiring bank, who passed it along to the merchant. Meanwhile, the customer waited angrily or was required to return later. The card-issuing bank posted a hold on the customer account for the amount of the sale, to be released when the sales draft appeared weeks, often months, later.

Merchants swiftly realized it was prudent to obtain an authorization in advance for every potential sale, however slight the chance it would be completed. Customers' lines of credit were swiftly absorbed by holds for sales never completed and they were denied credit they should have had. System authorization costs soared since merchants made local calls, while banks absorbed all long-distance bank-to-bank calls.

There was no Internet, no electronic entry of data, no CRT screens for electronic examination of accounts, and no dispersed computing power. All data entry required keypunching each digit of information (every letter and every number) into a four-by-six inch piece of cardboard by a clunking mechanical punching typewriter the size of a large refrigerator. The punched cards were then put through an elongated card reader twice the size of the keypunch machine to capture the data on magnetic tape, then fed into a van-sized computer for posting to customer accounts. The data were returned to tape and finally sent into a large mechanical printer to produce huge binders of customer records.

Primitive and cumbersome as the system was, it performed well enough to allow the massive outpouring of cards to gain considerable consumer and merchant acceptance. As acceptance skyrocketed, the number of transactions flowing between banks exploded. The clearing system swiftly disintegrated under the volume.

Very few bankers had sound experience in the management of unsecured consumer credit, and fewer had knowledge of credit cards. The most experienced and best-qualified people outside the banking industry were repelled by the methods and madness of the industry. However, there was no shortage of those with questionable ability and experience. They came forward in droves. Most were quickly snapped up.

Within the banks, similar problems appeared. Most bankers looked down their noses at the card business, placing it lower on the scale of respectability than auto dealer financing. Few banks really wanted to be in the card business. Few bankers wanted to be assigned to it. Card operations were located in the least desirable part of the bank premises and staffed with employees who did not fit elsewhere.

With problems mounting the situation was getting out of control of BofA...

1.1.2. Part Two

By 1968, the fledgling industry was out of control. No one knew the extent of the losses, but they were thought to be in the tens of millions of dollars, a huge sum for the time and for the size of the system.

In the midst of the credit card mess, the Bank of America Service Corporation called a meeting of licensee card program managers to discuss operating problems plaguing the system. Jim Cronkhite, operations officer of our card center, and I flew to Columbus, Ohio, to join one hundred twenty others from across the country. We were surprised to find that top officers of the BofA Service Corporation had apparently not thought it important to attend. Others were no less surprised. The meeting was to be conducted by Hal and Don, both pleasant and capable bank operations officers assigned to the Service Corporation to work with licensee banks.

The meeting droned on for most of the first day, many licensees sharply critical of what they perceived as the Bank of America's lack of awareness of the problems, and inability or unwillingness to deal with them. The Bank representatives were no less critical of their licensees. By the end of the day, accusations, denials, and counter-accusations were flying about the room.

The next morning was worse. By midday, the meeting disintegrated in acrimonious argument. Shortly before lunch, in evident desperation and without prior discussion with those named, Hal and Don announced appointment of a committee of seven licensee card-center managers, of which I was one, to which they intended to refer a couple of the more critical operating problems. We were to study the assigned problems and suggest solutions. If BofA found the suggestions agreeable, they would attempt to impose them on the licensee banks.

This was a turning point in the history of Visa. Dee Hock did not want to participate in the committee, because he thought such a committee would be an exercise in futility. During the lunch break, he asked Hal and Don for a few moments in private:

"Look, I don't want to make things more difficult than they already are. If you insist, I'll do this committee thing, but I'd rather not be involved. It would be a big favor if you'd get someone else."

Hal's reply is abrupt and sarcastic.

"You guys seem to think everything we try to do is wrong, so here's your chance to do it right."

Don is a bit more reserved but equally concerned.

"Dee, why not? Do you have a problem with the idea of the committee itself, or is there some other reason?"

It is a sheer waste of time. By the time the committee can meet and agree on anything, there'll be a dozen more problems. No one really knows how many problems there are or how serious they might be. Nothing a committee could suggest would satisfy everybody. The way your license agreements are written, if a bank refuses to go along with the rules, your only choice is to kick them out of the system. BofA won't do that and we all know it. It would jeopardize too many banking relationships.

"If you're going to form a committee," I reply, "why not give it responsibility for creating some way to examine all problems in a systematic, continuous way? What's the point in trying to correct any problem if we're constantly guessing about its importance, what else needs to be done, and how they all connect and affect one another? And why mill around yapping at one another out of ignorance?"

During the discussion, Dee managed to persuade Hal and Don to create a committee that would address all the problems at once, and not just one at a time. BofA representatives had hard time accepting the proposed solution.

It is a perplexed group that assembles after lunch to find one of their own, myself, take the stage.

Dee suggested that the committee address a single problem—how to create a cohesive, coherent, self-organizing effort involving all licensees to examine all problems plaguing the system. Dee insisted that it should be an open effort committing no one, including BofA, to anything other than participation.

"How much will it cost?" someone in the audience asks.

"Nothing but some of your time and an occasional airplane ticket."

"What will it commit us to?"

"Nothing."

The audience, in the way of all disorganized groups faced with a proposal creating the illusion of progress but requiring no money or commitment, swiftly agreed. The meeting disbanded and the committee of seven met.

Fred James, a soft-spoken, laconic man of considerable influence from Memphis, Tennessee, was the first to speak.

"Well, I don't know what you got us into, but this is sure enough your idea. Unless somebody wants to argue, looks like you're the chairman."

And just so, I was elbowed into the lead.

The first meeting of the newly-founded committee took place in Seattle.

We arrived in Seattle with a rough concept of multiple, self-defined regions, each with four functional committees—operating, marketing, credit, and computer systems. Every card-issuing bank within each region would have a right to appoint a representative to each of their regional committees. A regional executive committee would be composed of the chairmen of the functional committees and any other individuals the four chairmen selected. Five national committees would be composed of the chairman of each committee in the seven regions. Everyone would be heard but no one could dominate.

Within the week, the concept was expanded to a set of proposals. The licensee committee appointed by BofA met in Atlanta, Georgia. After a day of discussion and modification, agreement was reached. The seven regions became eight. Each member of the group would return to his region, host a meeting of all licensee banks to share the concept, and, if successful, coordinate self-organization of regional committees. In the event the concept was not acceptable to all regions, the effort would be abandoned. If the effort were successful, the regional committees would elect their respective chairmen, each of whom would become a member of a comparable national committee. The present committee, selected by the Bank of America, would be replaced by the national executive committee.

We hoped that the committee structure would not only develop preliminary data about fraud, credit, operating, and technology problems, but assign priority to them and propose solutions to the most vexing. Bank of America would have an ex-officio member on each national committee. As sole owners of the service marks and the franchising company, BofA would have responsibility for implementing any proposals. Whether BofA could or would, and how, was anyone's guess.

Within six months, the complex of regional and national committees had self-organized. Hock was asked to serve as chairman of the Pacific Northwest regional executive committee It was thankless, unpaid, often unpleasant work that consumed a lot of time.

The complex of committees had but one redeeming quality: It allowed organized information about problems to emerge. It took only two cycles of meetings to realize that the problems were enormously greater than anyone imagined—far beyond any possibility of correction by the existing committees or the licensing structure—and growing at an astonishing rate. Losses were not in the tens of millions, as everyone had thought, but in the hundreds of millions and accelerating.

Suddenly, little a diamond in the dirt, there it lay. The need for a new concept of organization and a precarious toehold from which to make the attempt.

Just what was the nature of the business in which we were engaged? Was credit really the nature of our business? What was the essence of the transaction when a customer presented a sliver of plastic to a merchant? Clearly, it introduced a merchant willing to sell something to a prospective customer who might wish to buy it. In that regard, it was a substitute for a driver's license, social security card, government identity card, or other means of identification. Thus, the first primary function of the card was to identify buyer to seller and seller to buyer.

Clearly, it guaranteed that they could safely exchange value, the merchant delivering goods or services, and the customer signing a draw that the merchant could deposit for monetary credit. The seller would receive good funds in local currency and the buyer would be billed later in the currency of their country. Thus, the second primary function was as guarantor of the value data.

Clearly, it warranted to both buyer and seller that the system would attend to the mechanism of exchange without either having to know the language, laws, currency, customs, or culture of the other.

Dee Hock went to meet Mr. Carlson (the President of NBC) to describe his desperate situation: the leadership of the committee at present took perhaps a quarter or more of his time, but if something comes of the effort, it might be more than full time. If the system fails, the bank will suffer huge losses. Meanwhile, his salary and expenses are not paid by the committee. To this point, every bank has paid its own way. Surprisingly, Mr. Carlson let Dee continue as a vice president of the bank and head of the credit card department with full salary and all expenses paid, putting the resources of the bank at his disposal, and demanding no more than he treat NBC as he would treat the others.

"Well, young man, sometimes we just have to be good citizens." Then he asked the question with which he closes all meetings: *"Did the meeting serve your purpose?"*

With compelling need for a new organization, a precarious toehold from which to make the attempt, and now, the liberty to try, I suppressed my desire to control the future, and tried to create the conditions by which new concepts might emerge.

I thought long and hard about each member of the national executive committee, settling on three, each of whom seemed to have a good sense of who they were, an open, curious mind, generous spirit, and keen sense of humor. More important, none seemed inclined to either follow or lead a mob. Each moved to a rhythm of his own.

After sharing belief about the opportunity that might be hidden in the problems of the system, I asked if they would be willing to take a week or more of their time, isolate themselves completely, set aside all thought of the problems of the system and address a single question based upon a single assumption.

If anything imaginable was possible, if there were no constraints whatever what would be the nature of an ideal organization to create the world's premier system for the exchange of value?

After a bit of head shaking and eye rolling, they became intrigued and agreed—providing I would join them. It would have been a bitter disappointment had they not asked.

They decided to isolate themselves in Altamira Hotel, located on a hillside in Sausalito, California.

Lying awake the fourth night, Old Monkey Mind and I knew that no bank could create the world's premier system for the exchange of value. No hierarchal stock corporation could do it. No nation-state could do it. No known organization could do it. But what if a fraction of the resources of all the financial institutions in the world and a fraction of the ingenuity of all people who worked for them could be applied? Jointly they might do it, but how?

Thus the first postulates of the new organization were formulated:

What if ownership was in the form of irrevocable right of participation, rather than stock:?

rights that could not be raided, traded, bought, or sold, but only acquired by application and acceptance of membership

What if it were self-organizing, with participants having the right to self-organize at any time, for any reason, at any scale with irrevocable rights of participation in governance at any greater scale?

What if power and function were distributive, with no power vested in or function performed by any part that could reasonably be exercised by any more peripheral part?

What if governance was distributive, with no individual, institution, or combination of either or both, particularly management, able to dominate deliberations or control decisions at any scale?

What if it could seamlessly blend cooperation and competition, with all parts free to compete in unique, independent ways, yet able to yield self-interest and cooperate when necessary to the good of the whole?

What if it were infinitely malleable, yet extremely durable, with all parts capable of constant, self-generated, modification of form or function without sacrificing its essential purpose, nature, or embodied principle, thus releasing human ingenuity and spirit?

It took months to develop and gain acceptance among licensees of the principles. Once accepted, they were the foundation of every discussion. They were accepted, in part, because no one, self included, thought it likely that such an organization could be brought into being.

The weeks after the Sausalito meeting were filled night and day by work with lawyers, accountants, and members of the various committees as we struggled to translate the principles into a conceptual structure. Dozens of working groups formed, dissolved, or combined as question after question was posed. No ultimate answers emerged, only better questions. If this institution were to self-organize, in effect, to design itself, it would require continual consensus. Not consensus in the modern meaning of unanimous agreement, but in the original, deeper sense of solidarity. A position where all could stand comfortably together to act in accordance with purpose and principle.

On June 24, 1969, the national licensee executive committee met in San Francisco for two days of intense work shaping the concept. Fred, Sam, Jack, and I met with Ken the third day to review our work, since an early response from the Bank of America was important to continuation of it.

Near the end of July, the reply came. "The bank is in sympathy with the avowed aims of your executive committee, namely to form a national association responsive to the collective needs and desires of the licensees but..." The bank then laid out its position. They must have representation on the board equal to their percentage of the sales volume. That would violate our fundamental principle of governance not dominated by any institution or interest. They must be retained as managing partner of the association for a minimum of five years. The bank, as managing partner, must retain ownership and control of all trademarks and remain as exclusive licensing agent, which it would exercise with dispassion and objectivity (presumably, an equitably elected board of a new organization could not do so). Again, it was contrary to all our principles.

The licensee executive committee assembled to consider whether to proceed with the reorganization in view of the bank's position. With the committee's consent, Dee called Ken Larkin, informing him that the committee was in session and before making a decision would like to go over the bank's position to be certain it was not based on misunderstanding of their work, or their misunderstanding of the bank's intent. Ken was adamant. To this, Dee said that his strong recommendation to the committee will be to abandon the effort and inform the media about BofA's decision. The answer to that comes after prolonged silence: *"Before you do that, perhaps you should come to San Francisco and meet with Sam Stewart, vice chairman of the board".*

A well-known lawyer who had won numerous lawsuits, Sam Stewart was number two officer in the largest bank in the world. Their meeting kicked off with Sam Stewart setting forth the position of the bank. It became apparent to Dee that he was there for correction, not conversation.

"The bank had pioneered the bank card business, they had created

BankAmericard—they had suffered through huge losses to make it profitable—they had created the licensing structure— major problems were normal in such an expansion—banks had taken licenses in reliance on the Bank of America's experience and expertise—the name BankAmericard, the name of the bank, and the goodwill of both were at stake—they had been cooperative throughout the organizational effort—they had made many concessions—it was unreasonable to expect them to subject themselves to a new, untested concept with unknown management—it was unreasonable to abandon the effort and blame the bank—we should accept their proposal and work in good faith to resolve system difficulties."

"Mr. Stewart, it's not politic or sensible for a vice president of a modest bank in Seattle to tell the vice chairman of the largest bank in the world that he is mistaken, but I believe you are." "What you propose is not in the best interests of the Bank of America, the licensees, or the industry."

"You really believe that, don't you?"

"Yes, sir, I really do."

"Then tell me why."

"Control of management would ensure the failure of a new organization—it was contrary to all the principles we had worked so assiduously to develop, in which we deeply believed—the new organization would have no heart, no spirit if they were abandoned—truly honest people would not work under such controlled conditions—the licensing structure could never compel cooperative behavior—licensees would never surrender autonomy to an organization controlled by one bank—reconceiving product and organization could expand the market for cards far beyond anything now imagined—the Bank of America would benefit far more from its share of that market than it ever could from royalties in the present market—the bank should be the leader of a movement, not the commander of a structure."

"Will you put your thoughts in writing and send them to me? Can you come again in two weeks?"

"Yes, sir."

Two days later, a three-page letter was in the mail to Sam. Two weeks later Dee returned to San Francisco. Sam met him at the door with a warm smile:

"We've thought very carefully about what you said and have come to the conclusion that, in the main, it is right. There are many things to be better understood and some to be negotiated, but you'll have our full support in the attempt to form a new organization in accordance with your principles, and our good faith in negotiating terms and conditions for transfer of ownership.

Understanding of the opportunities and excitement about the concepts were soon contagious

Early in 1970, it appeared everything was falling in place. The greatest obstacle of all could no longer be ignored At that time, there were more than 200 full-licensee card-issuing banks. Each had the right to sublicense other banks as agents to help them enroll merchants and solicit consumers for cards. Nearly 2,500 agent banks had been sublicensed. Meanwhile, the bank card frenzy had not subsided. Banks continued to flood into the business, fearing their traditional banking business would be eroded. Problems throughout the systems continued to accelerate.

The committee had to somehow induce more than three thousand banks to surrender their license for cancellation to Bank of America and simultaneously bind themselves to membership in a new organization quite unlike any that had existed before. It was to be called National BankAmericard Incorporated (NBI). It was a surrender of autonomy to their collective selves, since they would be the owners, members, and governors of the new organization.

Hock faced a difficult task. On the advice of Mr. Carlson, Hock decided to start with ten or fifteen of the most influential, highly respected chief executive officers whose lead will be followed.

It was an impressive group that met February 8, 1970, in New York in an awesome board room near the top of another towering bank headquarters. They greeted one another as old friends, comparing private jet flights, golf scores, and banking deals made. It was an intimidated sheep who sat silently, wondering if they were the kind of corporate people that bloodied the hides of obstreperous sheep. Nothing had prepared me for this, save a few conversations with Sam Stewart and Max Carlson. I'd never before been in a corporate board room. Little more than a year before, I had been sorting trash in the basement of a bank branch.

Sam opened the meeting and made it clear the Bank of America was receptive to the concepts but would act only as one of the group. Thereafter, he seemed content to sit quietly listening to others and observing their reaction, forcing me to handle the discussion and respond to concerns. The Chairperson opened the meeting.

It was clear the bank wanted freedom to act as it thought best after knowing the reaction of others. While he made no effort at persuasion, his mere presence and leadership in calling the meeting was enough to ensure a fair hearing from everyone. They were uniformly courteous, interested, perceptive—but noncommittal. Questions were to the point, and discussion centered on substantive issues rather than detail. My tension melted as I got out of myself and into the ideas that meant so much to me.

They left with the package in hand, committed only to meet thirty days later in Chicago. Meanwhile, they would receive a final package of proposals and documentation. In Chicago, after another half day of discussion, they would be asked to commit their bank or withdraw. If committed, they would agree to serve for another six months, and sponsor meetings of CEOs of full-licensee banks in their area at which the same presentation would be made. The proposal would live or die on its merits. Momentum was building.

March 11, 1970 is a raw, windy day in Chicago when the executive officers organizing committee gathers for the second time. Another towering bank building, another awesome board room, another splendid lunch. It's hard to imagine these folks ever meeting in a stockroom to sit on a box and laugh together over a sandwich. They are really comfortable in such posh places. I'm sure as hell not. But this is where life has led and there's nothing to be done about it.

The meeting begins with sharp, penetrating questions. No one appears to have taken the proposal lightly. I have no time to coddle my discomfort.

"What happens if a bank decides not to join?"

"The organizing principles require they not be left in a lesser position. Their license with Bank of America will remain in full force and effect. Members of the new organization will be obliged to interchange with them on the same basis as they would with other members. The Bank of America will apply all regulations adopted by NBI to the licensees. However, they will have no voice in the new organization."

"What if a bank decides not to join and does not wish to continue in the system?"

"They will be free to surrender their license, have ample time to discontinue operations, sell their program to another licensee, or

convert their BankAmericards to a competitive program of their choice."

"Will NBI be formed if only a small percentage of banks agree to join?"

"No." If two-thirds commit it will become operational. We believe NBI is important enough to risk losing participants that produce a third of the volume of the system, but not more. If members producing two-thirds of the volume do not join, the effort will be abandoned."

"What if the owner-members want to make major changes, such as selecting a new name and abandoning the name 'BankAmericard'?"

"There will be no restrictions on the power of the board to act in any manner within the constraints of law. However, the constitution of the new organization requires higher percentages of approval on such critical matters. The name can be changed if 80 percent of the banks approve."

"What assurance do we have that NBI can resolve present problems and create the kind of markets you envision?"

"None! It's a matter of judgment and trust."

The questions continue fast and intense, hour after hour.

In the middle of the afternoon, the questions dwindle and come to an end. Finally, the moment of truth. Will they commit their bank? Will they put their individual power and prestige behind the effort? They hesitate, then, surprisingly, ask if I will leave the room so they can have a half hour in private. There is no choice but to accede to their wishes. It is a half hour of torment.

The door finally opens and the reason is revealed. They have one condition without which none is prepared to make a commitment. There must be no change of leadership at this critical juncture. Will I commit to continue to lead the effort? It is puzzling. Why in the world would that require private discussion?

"Yes, of course. There is no way I will walk away until the job is done and the organization formed, even if it takes a year or more."

One of the more outspoken interjects.

No, you didn't understand! We want a commitment that you are prepared to move to San Francisco and head NBI. You've led the effort since the beginning and brought it this far. We don't want to risk a change of leadership during the remainder of the process, or for *several years thereafter. If you are willing, Sam will negotiate terms and conditions. Only the board of the new organization can appoint officers of NBI, but if they select you, we want to be certain you will accept. If you will make that commitment, you will have our commitment."*

- How? "All of you? Everyone?"

Yes.

This is how Visa was born. However there was still a lot of work ahead.

1.1.3. Part Three

As Old Monkey and I walked out of the woods with the maple cane and the journal, the choice was extremely difficult, yet simple. Either say no, abandon the dream or say yes and wholeheartedly accept the consequences, whatever they might be. With a heavy heart, but convinced it was the right decision, I returned to write a letter to Sam Stewart, mentioning but two needs: a salary small in relation to the responsibility and difficulty of the job ahead, but a bit more than our present income, and three years salary guaranteed should they wish me to step aside, or move the headquarters east of the Rocky Mountains. The modest salary was suggested to make it clear this was a labor of love, not a matter of money. I fully expected that Sam and the committee would insist on more generous terms. The three years was based on conviction that if I faced without equivocations the decisions and acts necessary to restore stability to the system I would so alienate members that continuance beyond three years would be impossible.

A week later, I met with Sam to discuss the letter. Sam was a lifelong employee and an integral part of the culture of the Bank of America. A. P Giannini, the founder of Bank of America, gained fame by living in the same modest, suburban house throughout his life and paying himself a small salary. Salary scales in the bank went down from there. Whether he did so from conviction, or as a means of keeping costs low, was never known. At the very least, it was disingenuous, for he enjoyed vast wealth from his shares in the bank and a host of amenities from organizations and foundations he controlled, while few employees had any. Whatever A. P's motives, as the growth of California in the first half of the century pushed the bank to prominence as the largest, most profitable in the world, it was equally prominent for abysmally low salaries. Sam is blunt.

"Dee, as President and CEO of NBI, your salary will be public information. There are only a half dozen people in the Bank of America who make as much as the salary you suggest. If NBI pays that salary it will become known in the bank, causing considerable discontent, and personal difficulty for me. We would be comfortable with a salary of $44,000 a year, beginning with the formation of NBI. We are also prepared to make a one-time payment of $10,000 in recognition of all that you have done in the past year and a half and must do in the months ahead to persuade the banks to join NBI and bring it into being."

Really? He can't be serious! Forty-four thousand dollars, no benefits and no equity to straighten out a $2 billion dollar mess? Ten thousand dollars for two years of innovation and grinding work against impossible odds? Only a half dozen people in the Bank of America who make $60,000 a year? Even if true, what of stock options, other benefits, perquisites, and lifetime security? But Sam is serious. He senses my distress and tries to ease the situation.

"Dee, these things take time. There was a period, earlier in my career with the Bank of America, when I went for years without a raise. It wasn't easy, but it worked out in the end."

"Sam, if that is true, the Bank was undoubtedly in error the second year, the third year, and every year thereafter. Have you discussed this with other members of the CEO organizing committee?"

"No. They authorized me to handle the matter. It should be settled here and now if we want their commitment."

Had I misjudged this man? What possible motive could underlie this absurdity? Even if what he says is true, why should my compensation be determined by the bias of a single man in a single bank? I refuse to believe this man dishonest or insincere. Mistaken, yes! Deceitful, no! I had not expected unpleasant circumstances to arrive so quickly or my convictions to be so rudely tested, but my decision had been made without equivocation, and so it would remain.

"Sam, I'll do as you wish. But don't ask me to agree with you. You're wrong again, but this time it only compromises my pocketbook, and I can live with that. Tell the committee yes and accept their commitment. I'll be back in a week with a plan.

As I left for Seattle, his pleasure seemed genuine and immediate.

When I returned a week later with the promised plan, Sam did not like it.

"Dee, it's impossible. There is absolutely no way three thousand banks can be persuaded to surrender their licenses, become members of NBI, hold an annual meeting of members, elect a board, and have the whole thing in operation in ninety days. It can't be done."

"Sam, we can't know that without making the attempt. We have the support of thirteen powerful people. We have the interest and participation of dozens of others who have worked on it for a year and a half. The concepts are sound. Momentum is building. If we link people in the right relationships, challenge them, and free them, they'll perform miracles. I've seen it happen before. Never on this scale, but we've got to try. If we drag it out it may never happen." Sam begins to waver. The time is now.

Dee asked BofA to contribute six or eight dedicated people for sixty days to process the surrender and cancellation of all licenses, a dozen experienced, willing people from card, legal, marketing, and systems departments, for six to eight months, to work solely in the interests of NBI and its prospective members, and a $200,000 line of credit for organizational expense. The NBI would be located in the vacant part of an old building across the street at reasonable month-to-month rent

" Do I know him well enough? Can I take the risk? It's irresistible. I rephrase his words from our salary discussion and give them back to him.

"Sam, there's no time to 'look into' these things. The operating committees authorized me to handle the matter. It should be settled here and now if we want their commitment.

" He laughs, paraphrases my words, and makes return.

"OK, we'll do as you wish. I'll accept and never say more—but don't ask me to agree with you. You're wrong. There is no way this will be done in ninety days. Tell your operating committees 'yes' and accept their commitment. I'll be back with a plan for the bank's part in a week.

Within a day after meeting with Sam, I called each member of the executive officers organizing committee with a brash request. Would each arrange a half-day, morning meeting with senior executive officers of each full-licensee bank in his region? Would each attend the meeting he had arranged, explain the work of the committee, and its commitment to the concept? The chairmen of the regional working committees and I would attend each meeting and present the proposal.

Would each accept an equal share of the organizational expense if the effort failed? It caught their fancy and all agreed.

They were as good as their word. Within ten days, they had coordinated with one another and twelve meetings were arranged, each on consecutive days at locations less than two hours flight time apart on well-traveled air routes.

In another ten days, I lifted off from the Seattle airport on the first leg of an impossible schedule. It's all a blur now—meeting after meeting—intense questions, skepticism, enthusiasm, criticism, confusion, persuasion—mad dashes to airports—catchas-catch-can sleep—no time, no time—twelve days, twelve cities, two hundred banks, hundreds of people. One event followed another.

The executive officers of the licensee banks were to take their copy of the certificate of incorporation, bylaws, license cancellation agreement, membership agreement, and operating material, review it with anyone they wanted, then send suggestions, if any, for improvement to the executive working committee, which would make final decisions for incorporation of essential changes. A final owner/member charter package would then be created and simultaneously sent to each bank, each containing a provision for acceptance within a charter period of thirty days acer receipt. Not a sentence, not a word, not a comma of the final charter package would be changed. Accept or reject—no other alternative, although membership would be open to any qualified bank at any time thereafter should the organization come into being.

Every bank electing to join would sign an identical, brief agreement in duplicate original, acknowledging receipt of the material and committing to abide by all provisions of the documents "as they now exist and are hereafter modified." A threshold of acceptance was specified. If reached, all charter member agreements and all contracts between NBI and the Bank of America would immediately be in full force and effect. If the threshold was not reached, all membership agreements and contracts would be null and void. A first meeting of owner/members was scheduled shortly after the deadline, at which the governing board would be elected and officers appointed, providing the effort was successful.

Each member would have one vote for every thousand dollars of sales volume transacted by their BankAmericard customers in the preceding year. Service fees would be one-quarter of 1 percent of that same sales volume. Thus, taxation and representation would be linked. Dividends *or distributions, if any, would be on the basis of that fraction of the service fees paid by any member to that paid by the total membership. There would be no need for endless negotiating, endless contracting, endless disputes, and legal battles. Essential rights and obligations, as well as the structure itself, would be self-organizing and self-governing in perpetuity.*

Memberships would be nontransferable and disconnected from cards and receivables. Portfolios of business could be bought and sold, but not owner/membership in the organization or rights to use of service marks or other properties. Those rights could only be acquired by eligibility, application, and acceptance to membership. However, it would be no closed club. Directors could determine general eligibility for membership but would have no power to decline any applicant meeting those requirements, or any power to accept an applicant who did not.

Although voting rights would be related to size of the program, there would be a one-bank, one-director rule. No matter how many votes a member acquired as a result of sales volume, once an employee of that bank was elected to the board, votes could not be used to elect another. Once elected, each director would have legal and fiduciary responsibility to the whole of the system, not to their bank or to the constituency from which elected. Each director would have a single vote with respect to board decisions.

There would be different types of directors. The country was divided into regions, each of which would elect a director. Only members headquartered in that region could vote for that region's directors. Five directors at large would be elected by the entire membership under cumulative voting procedures. One director would be elected by the smallest banks. Any bank having more than 15 percent of the sales volume could appoint a director.

Every director must be re-elected every year. The board could appoint a nominating committee to suggest candidates for election. However, if any other individual was nominated by a member and seconded by another, the person must be put on the ballot and given equal treatment with board nominees. Elections for regional directors could be by mail, but if a single member requested a meeting for purposes of election it must be held. Nominations could be made from the floor by any member at any meeting.

The president, appointed by the board, would be the chief executive officer and a member of the board by right of that appointment, but could not hold the chairmanship. The chairman would be elected by the board, but would have no executive or operating authority. The president would be responsible for preparing the agenda for board meetings. Any matter could be put on the agenda by any director. The chairman would preside at all board meetings, make certain all views were openly, equitably heard, and that decisions were in accordance with all provisions of the bylaws and policies of the organization, and relevant laws and regulations. The chairman would be free of any responsibility to support the views of management, and would have no right to suppress them.

Visa could not be bought, raided, traded or sold, since ownership was in the form of perpetual, nontransferable, rights of participation. However, that portion of the business created by each member was owned solely by that company, was reflected in its stock prices, and could be sold to any other member or entity eligible for membership—an extremely broad, active market.

Any member could retain full rights of membership in perpetuity if it issued a single Visa product to a single customer. However, the right to issue any and all products at any time, in any amount, in any area in accordance with complete freedom to determine services, prices, terms, conditions, and marketing, is subject only to minimum standards necessary for reciprocal acceptance of all cards.

The system became enormously robust, since virtually all innovation occurred in individual banks that formed the periphery of the system. Mistakes died quickly without affecting more than a single bank, while successes were swiftly emulated and improved upon as they spread throughout the system. While the core of the organization could develop products and services to be offered by members, it had no power to require that any member issue or promote any of them. Thus, central mistakes died as quickly and harmlessly as peripheral ones.

Its products were among the most universally used and recognized in the world, yet the organization was so transparent its ultimate customers, most if its affiliates, and some of its members did not know it existed or how it functioned. At the same time, the core of the enterprise had no knowledge of, information about or authority over a vast number of the constituent parts. Visa had multiple boards of directors within a single legal entity, none of which could be considered superior or inferior, as each had irrevocable authority and autonomy over geographic or functional areas.

No part knew the whole, the whole did not know all the parts, and none had any need to. The entirety, like millions of other chaordic organizations, including those we call body, brain, forest, ocean, and biosphere, was self-regulating.

A staff of less than five hundred scattered in more than a dozen countries on four continents coordinated this system.

I could think of no way to fully realize the concept by including merchants and cardholders as owner/members. The slightest hint in that direction raised a storm of opposition. We should have included them. Perhaps, with more time, tenacity, and ingenuity we could have. But that can never be known.

I had neither the experience nor strength of character to hold my convictions inviolable or develop them fully. I never ceased to try, but failed to properly keep at bay the four beasts that inevitably devour their keeper: ego, envy, avarice, and ambition. Today, as I continue to struggle with those same beasts, hundreds of thousands, perhaps millions of other people have done, and will do better.

The end of the beginning was drawing to a close. The first annual meeting of members of National BankAmericard Incorporated was at an end. All business on the agenda had been covered. Relieved to have survived the ordeal, I asked the rhetorical question,

"Is there any other business to come before the meeting?"

Sam Stewart rose to his feet, stern and unsmiling. His booming voice filled the auditorium.

"Yes, there is. I have some unfinished business."

Oh my God, what now, I thought, as Sam faced the audience and began.

"When the Bank of America agreed to support the attempt to form NBI, we were convinced a quarter of the licensees would drop out. When Dee insisted we must perfect the new organization and convert the entire system in ninety days, I told him there was absolutely no way it could be done. " He paused for effect and with great emphasis boomed, " I just want you to know I haven't changed my mind one bit!"

The meeting dissolved in laughter and ended. You have to love a man like that. The newly elected board met, elected Sam chairman, and appointed me president and chief executive officer. Thus began what I expected would be a three-year commitment before I could regain a measure of freedom and return to a more private life in the Northwest. Had I an inkling those three years would become fourteen, or of the trials and trauma that lay ahead, I would have walked away on the spot.

The bank had been in secret discussions with American Express for months. They had jointly developed a plan for the two companies to build a nationwide credit card authorization system, to be owned and controlled by the two of them. At the time, American Express, by a huge margin, was the largest travel and entertainment card issuer in the world. Bank of America, by a similar margin, was the largest bank card issuer. Other credit card issuers would be invited to become participants in the new system, each paying a substantial sum at the time of commitment, which would provide most of the capital for development of the authorization system. However, they would have no ownership. The plan would be announced within days.

I felt completely betrayed. It was contrary to the spirit of the effort to form NBI and could materially affect its success. Throughout the effort to form NBI, all participants, including those from Bank of America, had agreed that one of the principal reasons for its formation was to create an effective means of authorizing credit card transactions. The joint venture, from my perspective, was nothing but an attempt by the two credit card giants to make tenant farmers of the remainder of the industry. In fairness, their effort may have been underway before it was certain NBI could be brought into being. I felt helpless.

The board meeting at which the decision was taken was unforgettable. We proposed that NBI break with the industry, withdraw from the joint effort, and announce intent to build a proprietary, competitive system for the electronic authorization of sales and the clearance of transactions and payments. There followed intense discussion among twenty-two powerful directors with diverse, strongly held opinions. It was far more important than any decision we had yet made. Failure meant risking the reputation of the new company, its ability to attract new members, its opportunity to undertake major ventures, and its financial stability.

The next day we shocked the industry with an announcement that NBI was withdrawing from the industry-wide effort and would build its own competitive, proprietary system. We were off the high dive. There was no way back. The only question was how we would hit the water.

It was a horrendous belly flop. Fail is exactly what we did. With very little experience among the staff, we had agreed it would be prudent to hire a systems development expert from outside the company. Within days, our expert persuaded us to follow tradition, write a request for *proposal and put it out to bid with leading development companies. It seemed sensible enough. It seemed sensible enough. As the weeks went by, I became a little nervous. The "expert" leading the effort continually assured me all was well, but seemed reluctant to share much information, claiming he wanted to be certain of his facts before making a final recommendation. Well, trust is not negotiable. One either trusts or one does not. I prefer trust.*

Eventually, the day came. The best bid from a responsible vendor was several times the anticipated amount approved by the board. The system would take twice as long as expected to build. No vendor was willing to warrant the performance of the system that might result. It was not a problem in the mind of the expert or the vendors. We should go back to the board and ask for more money and time. It was customary in the computer industry. Well, it was not going to become a custom at NBI. Some lessons must be learned over and over again before they sink to the bone. Emerson said it best. "Trust thyself; every heart vibrates to that iron string."

The people involved in the effort were brought together, everyone, inside and outside the company, at every level. There was little that needed to be said.

"We're told the system can't be built within the time and with the money we expected, some of which we have already wasted. If it can, it's clearly up to us. There is no answer out there. If there is an answer, it's in here. It's in us. We can go back to the board for more money and time, or we can believe that there is more than enough intelligence, ability, and ingenuity in this room to do the job. If there are enough of us with sufficient desire and trust in one another, we can close the door and not come out until we have decided how to meet our commitment within the promised time and with the money remaining."

Intense, innovative discussion erupted. There were more than enough excited, committed people, but the "expert" was not among them. He quietly went his way. Several exceptional people working for vendors leaped at the challenge and joined the company. We shut ourselves in a room and didn't come out until we had an approach to which we were totally committed. We called it Bank Authorization System Experimental (BASE 1). The following months were among the most exciting in the early history of the company. We were determined that the needs of our members and cardholders would be served, not the needs of technology or vendors. That required internal responsibility. We decided to become our own prime contractor, farming out selected tasks to a variety of software developers, then coordinating and implementing results. Conventional wisdom held it to be one of the worst possible ways to build computerized communications systems.

Swiftly, self-organization emerged. An entire wall became a pin board with every remaining day calendared across the top. Someone grabbed an unwashed coffee cup and suspended it on a long piece of string pinned to the current date. Every element of work to be done was listed on scraps of paper with the required completion date and name of the person who had accepted the work. Anyone could revise the elements, adding tasks or revising dates, providing they coordinated with others affected. Everyone, any time, could see the picture emerge and evolve. They could see how the whole depended on their work, and how their work was connected to every other part of the effort. Groups constantly assembled in front of the board as need and inclination arose, discussing, deciding, and forming work groups in continuous flow, then dissolving as needs were met. As each task was completed, its scrap of paper would be removed. Each day, the cup and string moved inexorably ahead.

No one ever forgot the joy of bringing to work the wholeness of mind, body, and spirit; discovering in the process that such wholeness is impossible without inseparable connection with others in the larger purpose of community effort.

Money was a small part of what happened. The effort was fueled by a spontaneous expansion of the nonmonetary exchange of value—things done for one another without measurement or prescribed return—the heart and soul of all community. The people gave of themselves without expectation and received in ways beyond calculation. A few who could not adjust to the diversity, complexity, and uncertainty wandered away. Dozens volunteered to take their place. No one articulated what was happening. No one recorded it. No one measured it. But everyone felt it, understood it, and loved it.

The dirty string was never replaced and no one washed the cup. "The Dirty Coffee Cup System" became legendary—a metaphor within the company for years to come. The BASE 1 system came up on time, under budget, and exceeded all operating objectives. It forced the industry to abandon notions of natural monopoly, innovate, and create other systems. It was a foundation of commitment and practice from which the global Visa communication systems evolved. Out of initial failure, grew a magnificent success.

Simultaneously, NBI placed a moratorium on dual membership. In other words, NBI member banks could not join similar organizations.

MasterCharge, the principal competitor, then larger than NBI, had publicly announced that they did not share these views and had no intention of adopting a similar prohibition

There were compelling arguments on both sides of the issue. Banks that wished to join both systems argued that an NBI prohibition of dual owner/membership would infringe on their freedom to offer any products they wished to consumers and merchants, thus restraining bank-to-bank competition. No one denied that prohibition of dual membership would place some constraint on bank behavior. But was that a necessary restraint in order to ensure the emergence of new systems and foster even greater competition? I, along with many others, thought that it was.

Was prohibiting institutions from becoming owner/members in competing systems an essential restraint to foster the emergence of many systems and ensure maximum competition between them, as well as between banks?

"If we do not prevent duality now, there will never be more than two bank card systems. Pressure to diminish their competitive vigor, perhaps even to merge the two will never end. The precedent will roll over into debit cards and other payment systems. It's not a matter of proof, it's a matter of common sense."

However, the antitrust division of the Department of Justice did not support Dee Hock and his team.

It is conceivable that two, at most three payment system behemoths may straddle the Earth and that a handful of member financial institutions will control boards and management of all three. It need not have been so in the past. It should not be so now. It might become worse in the future. It ought not to be so, ever.

To this day I often have regret I did not screw my courage to the sticking point and fight on: go down then and there, unbowed and unrepentant. To this day I wonder if the implied death threats affected my courage and judgment. Whether removing the prohibition of duality was a prudent act or a failure of courage and judgment I shall never know.

1.1.4. Part Four

As NBI struggled with duality, communications systems, marketing, security, and other major efforts required to turn the BankAmericard system around in the United States, the Bank of America Service

Corporation continued to license banks in the remainder of the world. Each license was different, leading to a morass of different marketing, computer systems, operations, and names. The blue, white, and gold card known as BankAmericard in the United States was known as Sumitomo Card in Japan, Barclaycard in the United Kingdom, Chargex in Canada, Bancomer in Mexico, and a multitude of other names in different countries. The situation quickly led to even greater and more complex problems than those experienced earlier in the United States, partially due to the diversity of language, currency, culture, and legal systems.

Influenced by the formation of NBI, international licensees formed a committee and made an effort to create an international organization. The effort failed. Late in 1972, the international licensee committee requested that the management of NBI lead a second effort to form a worldwide organization. We were not averse to the idea, although it raised complex issues. How could NBI take the lead without extending the perceptions and experience of one culture into many others? That would be anathema to the remainder of the world, and properly so. How could we reconcile our clear obligation to act in the best interests of NBI members with an obligation to act in the best interests of banks outside the United States? Could we afford to divert time and energy from the many difficult problems in the United States? On the other hand, could we afford not to, since our success was irrevocably intertwined with the success of the program overseas? How could the ultimate dream of creating the world's premier system for the exchange of value be realized without an effective global organization?

The effort would be immensely more complex than NBI. A global organization would need to transcend diverse languages, cultures, currencies, customs, legal systems, political traditions, and technologies. It would involve thousands of banks scattered around the world, as well as national consortiums of banks in France, Canada, Scandinavia, Japan, the United States and other countries. It must anticipate that tens of thousands of diverse financial institutions in more than 200 countries and territories might wish to participate. It could easily take several years of effort with no assurance of success. Yet such an organization, if it could be created, would have a huge advantage in the U. S. market as well as the rest of the world. Clearly, the experience gained and trust developed in the formation of NBI would be invaluable. It was time for NBI to be a good global citizen

I approached the NBI board in the spirit of Maxwell Carlson, pointing out that management could not undertake the effort unless released *from its obligation to represent the interests of NBI.*

Nor could the effort succeed if we were without position, income, and ability to continue to lead NBI. Many of the NBI directors, including the chairman of the board, Sam Stewart, had been on the NBI executive officer organizing committee. They under-stood how important my independence from the National Bank of Commerce had been to the success of that effort. They knew how fiercely I had defended that independence, and the right of the various committees to act openly, in the best interests of all.

By board resolution, they authorized the management of NBI to act as organizing agent with freedom and obligation to act in the best interests of all parties worldwide. We were released from any obligation to act in the express interests of NBI in connection with the international organizing effort. The executive committee of the board was charged with representing NBI in the event of conflict of interest. It was an extraordinary act on the part of the NBI board of directors.

Thus began two years of simultaneous service as the president and chief executive officer of NBI, and as independent organizing agent on behalf of the international licensees. It was fascinating beyond description, filled with support, betrayal, and surprises beyond anything I could have imagined.

After two years of constant struggle we had resolved an incredible number of differences but three powerful disagreements remained. The conflicting positions had been adopted at the highest level of each licensee bank as a condition of their participation in the new organization. The differences seemed impossible to reconcile. The committee had agreed to a final day and a half meeting, after which the effort would be abandoned if positions had not changed. In conversations leading to the meeting, it became apparent that positions, rather than softening, had hardened. As organizing agent, we were desperate to think of a way to break the impasse. We could think of no compromise that had a chance of being accepted.

The process was no longer as open and honest as it ought to be. there were efforts to subvert formation of a new international organization Dee Hock announced that the management of NBI could no longer act as organizing agent. All agreed that nothing further could be done until after the annual meeting of all licensees. The annual meeting of all licensees in Spain would take place a few weeks hence

I had a lifelong habit of backing away from difficult situations and approaching them in a playful, unorthodox way. I gave up efforts to

find a compromise and began to reflect on the exceptional effort of the past two years and the progress that had been made. I began to peel the mental onion; to get at the essential nature of that which had lifted such a complex, diverse group over seemingly insurmountable obstacles. It was hard to get at, but simple when it emerged. At critical moments, all participants had felt compelled to succeed. And at those same moments, all had been willing to compromise. They had not thought of winning or losing, but of a larger sense of purpose and concept of community that had transcended and enfolded them all.

Several members of the staff joined in and within the hour, we had a plan. We reduced our thoughts to the simplest possible expression: the will to succeed, the grace to compromise. Conveying those principles in the living language of any member of the group was sure to give offense to others.. It must be in a dead language. A linguist was asked for a translation into Latin, which he rendered as Stadium ad prosperandum, voluntas in conveniendum. To this day I do not know the accuracy of his translation, nor does it matter, for it has taken on a meaning larger than the language itself.

We contacted a fine, local jeweler and asked that a die be created from which to cast sets of golden cufflinks. On one would be a half round of the Earth with continents in relief; circling it in raised letters, "Stadium ad prosperandum." The other cufflink would be the other half of the Earth and its continents, circled with "Voluntas in conveniendum." We had a set made for every member of the committee. We said nothing to anyone about what we had done.

The meeting convened on a splendid, warm day in San Francisco. It was polarized and cantankerous. The four large banks that composed Chargex in Canada were adamant. Unless others around the world accepted their demands they would not participate. In desperation, I looked around the group and asked,

"Well, it is obvious Canada cannot accept the position of others on this issue. Is it the sense of the group that you wish to proceed to form the new organization without our friends from Canada?

"Nods all around.

"Well, then, it appears Chargex representatives will no longer be part of the process. Would it be appropriate to have them remain as observers with the understanding they will not participate in remaining discussions?

"Again, nods all around. The Canadians were shocked, but did not *leave.*

Things got no better. There was adamant disagreement on the remaining issues. As the day ended, gloom deepened. I suggested we adjourn the meeting, since agreement appeared impossible. We could meet in the morning to disband the effort. Meanwhile, in recognition of their past extraordinary efforts, we wanted them to experience the finest that San Francisco had to offer. We boarded a private boat at Fisherman's Wharf for a trip across the bay to a fine French restaurant, Le Vivoire, in Sausalito. It was within a block of where Sam, Jack, Fred, and I met four years before to ask the impossible question, if anything imaginable was possible, if there were no constraints whatever what would be the nature of an ideal organization to create the world's premier system for the exchange of valued It seemed fitting to bury the idea where it had been born.

Mother Nature could not have been more generous. As the boat departed from Fisherman's Wharf, a magnificent sun was sinking behind the Golden Gate Bridge, painting huge, cumulus clouds over spectacular shades of pink and purple, turning the colossal bridge to its famous, flaming, golden color, bringing out the marvelous pastel hues of the city, and swathing the deep blue of the bay with a path of sparkling light from the boat to the horizon. It was shirtsleeve weather as the boat circled the fortress-like buildings of the former federal prison on Alcatraz Island, then slid past the lush green of Angel Island to dock among the quaint houseboats lining the shores of Sausalito.

After a short walk to the restaurant, a few bottles of fine wine, and a splendid dinner, it was a mellow group of people who faced me when I asked for a moment to say a few words before the evening ended. After reminiscing for a few moments about the many experiences we had shared, the obstacles overcome, and the exceptional effort expended, a small gift was placed before them as I concluded.

"It is no failure to fall short of realizing such a dream. From the beginning, it was apparent that forming such a complex, global organization was unlikely. We now know it is impossible, notwithstanding two years of exceptional effort. Not knowing with certainty how today's meeting might end, we felt compelled to do something that would be appropriate no matter what happened. Would you please open the small gift on the table before you?"

As they each opened a small, beautifully wrapped box and began to examine the contents, I quietly continued. "We wanted to give you something that you could keep for the remainder of your life as a reminder of this day. On one cufflink is half of the world surrounded with the Latin phrase, 'Studium ad prosperandum'—the will to succeed. On the second cufflink is the other half of the world surrounded with 'Voluntas in conveniendum'—the grace to compromise. We meet tomorrow for the final time to disband the effort after an arduous two years. There is no possibility of agreement. As organizing agent, we have one last request. Will you please bring your cufflinks to the meeting in the morning? When it ends, each of us will take them with us as a reminder for the remainder of our lives that the world can never be united through us because we lacked the will to succeed and the grace to compromise. But if, by some miracle, our differences dissolve before morning, this gift will remind us to the day we die that the world was united because we had the will to succeed and the grace to compromise."

There was a moment of profound silence as they examined their gift. It was shattered by one of my more exuberant Canadian friends, may his soul rest in peace, who rose with a huge grin and exploded,

"You miserable bastard!"

The room filled with laughter as the dinner ended.

The next morning, no one was without their cufflinks. Many committee members had been up much of the night calling officials of their bank or members of their constituency, demanding authority to reach agreement. The chairman was greeted by silence as he opened the meeting with a quiet question,

"Is there anyone who wishes to speak of disbanding the effort?" The Canadians immediately ceded their previous position in deference to the others and announced that they were to be part of the new organization. Within the hour, as individuals quietly touched one or the other of their cufflinks, agreement was reached on every issue.

When the international organization, then called Ibanco, now Visa International came into being a few months later, will to succeed, the grace to compromise became the corporate motto. As far as I know, to this day, every new director receives a set of the golden cufflinks and a parchment relating the story. Money could never compensate me for mine.

In 1973, it became apparent that continuing proliferation of names for the card could hinder growth of the system. At the time, the only common worldwide identity was the blue-whitegold bands design. The product had a different name in every country and in some countries, *several names. In the United States, the common name was BankAmericard. In Canada, Chargex. In the remainder of the world, it was usually known by the name of the issuer, such as Sumitomocard in Japan, or Barclaycard in the United Kingdom. Once the card had been introduced in the name of one bank, others were reluctant to join. The multitude of names was confusing to merchants, seriously undermining card acceptance. Ability to conduct international marketing and ensure acceptability of cards was severely limited.*

Merchant windows and counters were plastered with the name of the bank that contracted with the merchant for acceptance of cards. "Barclaycard Welcome Here." "Sumitomocard Welcome Here." Merchants resented commercialization of their premises by banks. Cardholders were often confused, thinking only cards of the named bank were acceptable, a misunderstanding some of the banks were not unhappy to perpetuate. As the system grew, so did the problem. In the United States, the name BankAmericard was limiting, as other banks were not happy promoting the identity of Bank of America. Savings and loan companies and credit unions gained legal authority to enter the business. They did not like the "bank" connotation of the name.. The "American" connotation of the card was not appreciated in other countries. "Card" was out of keeping with possible new products such as travelers checks and money orders. Each year that passed made solution of the problem more difficult. With the formation in June 1974 of Ibanco, the name chosen for the new international corporation, the whole of the enterprise finally had a governance mechanism capable of approaching such a vast, complex problem.

At the formation of Ibanco, another extraordinary event occurred. As the international committee turned its attention to management of the new corporation they were not anxious to lose the management that had seen them through the effort. Could there be common management between two such organizations? At first, it seemed impossible. They were two entirely different legal entities: National BankAmericard, composed of U. S. banks, and Ibanco, composed of several national consortiums such as NBI, Chargex, Carte Bleue, and hundreds of individual banks throughout the world.

On issue after issue, whether in marketing, service fees, operations, new products, or other areas, the interests of NBI members would oven differ from those of other Ibanco members. Conflicts of interest would be inevitable, yet that was exactly the case during the two years we acted as organizing agent to create Ibanco. We agreed to look into the matter.

An unusual agreement was devised. Ibanco and NBI would enter into a joint management agreement in which the same staff and officers would serve both organizations. Any officer could be terminated by either board, but it would take both to appoint them. Thus, management would be promoted and rewarded by joint agreement, but could be discharged or demoted by unilateral decision of either. In the event of a conflict of interest, management would be obliged to declare it, and announce which party they intended to represent. The other party would be represented by its board.

Soon after the formation of Ibanco we approached the board for authority to investigate adoption of a common, worldwide name. It was an awesome task for a new organization. Every card in the world would have to be reissued. Every merchant decal on every window and at every point-of-sale counter would have to be replaced. Every electronic sign would have to come down and be replaced—twenty thousand in Japan alone. Every form, every bit of stationery, and every sign in every bank would require replacement. All advertising would have to be changed. It would involve dozens of languages, cultures, and legal systems. No single center of authority or management group could ever hope to know, let alone understand, the full extent of the diversity and complexity involved.

Not only would such immense change have to occur, it could not be done in lockstep. It would have to be done by an incredibly diverse complex of thousands of independent institutions, each of which would need autonomy in making its part of the conversion. Each would need freedom to explain and market the change in competition with all others. Yet, it must happen swiftly and cooperatively, with equity and fairness. It must seamlessly blend cooperation and competition.

The situation was further complicated. Although Ibanco had obtained an exclusive license from the Bank of America for the blue-white-gold bands design, and the name BankAmericard, both were still owned by the bank. Fortunately, at the time of formation of Ibanco, we had negotiated an agreement compensating the Bank of America for surrender of ownership of the international part of the system. The agreement provided that should a new name be adopted acceptable to 80 percent of the system, ownership of the bands design would be transferred to Ibanco without additional compensation. Use of the name, BankAmericard, would be discontinued by all banks and revert to the Bank of America for its exclusive use.

We again turned to our growing habit of looking for underlying purpose and principle as the point of beginning. The purpose part was quite simple—to create a common, worldwide name for the organization and all its products to compliment the common blue-white-gold bands design, with ownership of both cooperatively vested in the totality. With no thought to what the new name might be, we began to create principles that it must embrace. One by one they emerged.

The new name must be short, graphic, and capable of instant recognition. It must be easily pronounceable in any language. It must have no adverse connotations in any language or culture. It must be capable of worldwide trademark protection for the exchange of value and all related activities. It must have no restrictive connotations, whether related to geography, institution, service or form, such as Ameri-, Euro-, bank, charge, credit, or card. It must have implications of mobility, acceptance, and travel. Before we were done, the list contained more than fifteen principles to which any new name must conform. It was daunting. We decided to simply release human ingenuity and see what happened.

We called the entire staff together, from the newest mail handler to management.

If they wished, anyone was free to participate in any way they found interesting and challenging, whether individually or in self-organized groups. A representative group would form to consider all suggestions and help formulate the best possible answer. There would be no consultants or outside experts. The employees were the experts, one and all. The person who came up with the answer would receive a munificent fifty-dollar check. Should it be a team effort that produced the result, each member of the team would have a check. The payment was purely symbolic. A large amount would produce a tendency to hoard ideas and information. Desire to have the check as a framed memento, in addition to the excitement and challenge of open participation, was compelling enough. We also have a moustache ourselves.

There was an explosion of ingenuity. The effort swiftly self-organized. Those technically inclined wrote software programs to fabricate names from letters of the alphabet. Family and friends were engaged. Dictionaries of roots and meaning in numerous languages were sifted and combed. I doubt anyone involved read, saw, or experienced anything in their daily lives without wondering if it might contain a clue to the answer. Great excitement arose each time someone thought they had solved the puzzle, only to be met with good-natured skepticism and challenge by others. Marketing people felt compelled to find the answer before someone in the mailroom beat them to it. Mailroom people felt challenged to demonstrate they were as creative as anyone in marketing, which many proved to be.

Lists of possibilities emerged, were combined in various ways, suggestions appearing and disappearing as the winnowing process continued. Hundreds of ideas emerged, failed to meet the test of purpose and principles, and were abandoned. Within months, no more than a handful remained. One, which had been discounted on the assumption it was so common it could never meet the test of trademark protection, continually reappeared and often rose to the top. VISA. Was it possible such a common name, used for centuries to denote an entry document to a foreign country, might be capable of trademark protection for financial services worldwide? Maybe, just maybe, it was so old and common that no one had thought of using it for financial services.

A worldwide trademark search was quietly undertaken to determine if it had ever been used in the field of financial services. One by one, the reports came in. There was a Visa car. There were Visa golf clubs. There were Visa fabrics. We held our breath. There were Visa pens. There were Visa appliances, there were Visa products of many kinds, but we could find no use of Visa for financial services, publications, or related activities of any significance. We quietly filed worldwide trademark registrations in every possible jurisdiction for the use of the name for financial and related services.

Whether or not we could gain worldwide acceptance for the change among our members was unlikely, but at least we had a beginning, a protected name to propose. But who was to get the fifty-dollar check? There were dozens of different recollections of where and how the name first appeared. No matter how hard we tried, none among us could unravel the puzzle. The name had appeared as an integral part of a self-organizing process. In a staff meeting to celebrate our success and untangle the puzzle someone wisecracked, "Maybe it suggested itself. Either make the check payable to 'everyone' or to 'no one'. It belongs to us all." Amid much laughter, the matter was settled.

It was at a meeting in Hawaii that the final decision would be taken. I was frantic to know how to bring everyone to the table in constructive agreement. The night before the meeting, as Ferol and I wandered alone along a path bordering the ocean, we noticed an enticing promontory and walked out to sit on a bench. Another couple appeared and asked if they might enjoy the sunset with us, to which we warmly agreed. We fell into pleasant conversation about the beauty of the spot *and the spectacular show Mother Nature was providing as the sunlight faded and stars emerged.*

The next day, as the meeting began, I discovered my acquaintance of the evening before, John Clinton, was a managing director of Barclay's bank, concerned enough to travel halfway around the world to persuade others that the name change was a wrongheaded notion. Discussions were intense, differences strong, and nothing resolved as the day progressed. In accordance with our custom, the meeting was adjourned early in the afternoon, so that people could mingle, privately share views, and enjoy the company of one another. John asked for a private word with me. We agreed to meet on the beach in an hour.

As we lay prone on the sand under a hot tropical sun, he explained with great clarity and depth why Barclay's bank simply could not accept the name change. I listened carefully, trying to put myself into his skin and see things through his eyes. Clearly, from his perspective, he was right. Were anyone in a similar situation, they would feel the same. There was no point in argument. On the other hand, had he put himself in the skin of others? Could he see with their eyes? Were other perspectives equally relevant to the interests of Barclay's bank?

I asked if he had time to listen to the perspectives of others, which I would try to convey. He readily agreed. I smoothed out a section of wet sand and began to sketch merchant decals and card layouts, illustrating the difficulties experienced worldwide and the opportunities presented by a common name. From one corner of my eye I could see a member of the NBI staff, signaling an urgent need to speak to me. I waved him away, since John was swiftly absorbing dimensions of the problem that had escaped his attention and I did not want to break the flow of conversation. My back was beginning to burn. I choked back a grin as the inevitable parental homily popped into mind: "It's no skin off my back." This may well be skin off mine. It was a small price to pay. Within the hour, John said,

"We may not have fully understood the issues. I want to think about this overnight and speak with others from Barclay's. We may be able to support the name change."

I thanked him and left.

The staff had bad news. Bernard Sue, head of Carte Bleue, had been roughly handled by some of the proponents of the name change. He had angrily announced he was returning to France on the next flight, would no longer participate in the meeting, and stormed away. It could easily disrupt the consensus that had been building.

"Where is Bernard?" I asked. "Has he left yet?"

Someone extended his arm, pointing to the ocean. At first, I could see nothing. As the swells rose, Bernard appeared, far out in the ocean.

My heart sank. A dinner meeting at which I must preside was but an hour and a half away. In his younger days, Bernard had been an Olympic-class swimmer. I was a country kid, reasonably at home in ponds and canals, but the ocean was another matter. I need to have a talk with you. I was determined Bernard must not leave. Duty calls in strange ways. There was nothing to do but to plunge in and slowly work my way out. Fortunately, Bernard was on his way in.

We met a hundred yards offshore, treading water as we spoke. It was a stroke of good fortune, for he was relaxed and in his element. We talked for more than half an hour, he breathing easily as I struggled to stay afloat. Whether it was pity for an awkward creature in distress or the calming effect of the great mother ocean is hard to say, but he was receptive and kind, agreeing that the importance of Carte Bleue to the system was too great to be jeopardized by unintended offense, no matter how egregious. He would set the matter aside and remain.

Good and bad fortune, like bananas, often come in bunches. At dinner that evening, I sat next to the representative from Sumitomo Bank in Japan. We fell into a deep discussion about bonsai, a hobby I was then clumsily pursuing. He was an expert in the field and gently told me of a bonsai tree handed down through five generations of his family. It was now in his custody. It gave him a profound sense of the continuity of life, the importance of honoring ancestors and the obligation to respect the needs of generations yet to be. When he traveled, he had concern about remaining too long, for he felt great personal responsibility for the tree. It must be passed to the next generation, healthy and enhanced. I shared with him my deep conviction that life is not a possession. Nor is life merely a contract between the living. Life is a sacred contract between the dead, the living, and the unborn.

Without intention on either part, the conversation drifted to Ibanco, the extraordinary relationships on which it was based, the sacrifices that had been made to bring it into being, and whether it too was a living thing that should be passed from generation to generation enhanced. We lapsed into silence, realizing a profound sense of shared responsibility. Not a word was said about our differences regarding the name change. Yet, in the beautiful, subliminal way that comes so easily in Eastern cultures, I had the feeling that we were becoming as one on the work to be done.

When it came time to make a few remarks to end the dinner, I asked his permission, then quietly shared the story he had told me about his family bonsai and concern for its welfare. I reminded the group that the Sumitomo family had originated as samurai warriors four hundred years earlier, migrating into the mining of copper, eventually into banking and a great many other businesses, adding:

"We should think carefully before we drag out our discussion tomorrow, put in jeopardy the life of such a tree, or arouse the samurai spirit of one who is responsible for its life."

He was smiling gently as I finished.

Indeed, people must come to things in their own time, in their own way, for their own reasons, or they never truly come at all.

One can never understand why things happen as they do. Perhaps it was no more than imagination, but discussions the next day seemed to have a different quality. They were no less intense and penetrating, yet had a subtle feel of desire for commonality rather than difference; a feel of something beyond self, nation, culture, or institution tugging at one's sleeve.

A unanimous decision emerged at that meeting to change the corporate name, Ibanco, to Visa International Services Association. The acronym, of course, was VISA. National BankAmericard became Visa USA. At the same time a unanimous decision was taken to change all products worldwide to the name Visa. Thus the corporate names and product names became one. Those decisions caused many individuals great trouble as they returned to explain to others within their institutions what had happened. It may have been detrimental to some of their careers, yet they made the decision and never turned back. Within weeks, plans were made for a four-year phase-in of the conversion to allow time for the complex work to be done. General objectives were established that allowed every institution complete freedom to make the conversion in any way it chose. There were no commandments, threats, or penalties. No member was told how to do anything. Instead, dates were agreed on by which they would be expected to reach certain objectives. Cardholders and merchants responded with enthusiasm, the conversion self-organized, and a year and a half later, there were few old cards, decals, or forms to be found. It was done in a third the time anticipated. Within another three years, Visa had surpassed all its rivals by a substantial margin.

1.2. Epilogue

In October 2007, Visa Inc. was established as a separate legal entity, with Visa USA, Visa International, Visa Canada and Inovant becoming its affiliates. Visa Europe did not become an affiliate, remaining in private ownership it is managed by European financial institutions, members of the association. In 2008 the company held an IPO. Currently, Visa shares are traded on the New York Stock Exchange. After holding IPO, Visa moved away from the original principles of decentralized management advocated by Dee Hock.

Visa is the world leader in the payment card market, accounting for 57% of this market.

Interestingly, Dee Hock today is on the advisory board of Xapo,[6] arguing that "We live in the 21st century but are still using command and control organizational structures from the 16th century. Bitcoin is one of the best examples of how a decentralized, peer-to-peer organization can solve problems that these dated organizations cannot."

1.3. The Evolution of MasterCard

BofA's decision to license banks to issue BankAmericard cards to their customers has eventually led to the formation of a single Interbank Cards Association (ICA), in 1966, bringing together several regional associations, which was the starting point for what later became known as MasterCard International.

INTERBANK

In 1966, 17 banks formed the Interbank Card Association (ICA), a new association with the ability tc exchange information on credit card transactions. Once the federation was formally established, the Interbank Cards Association (ICA) adopted the symbol "i" as its logo. Unlike other similar organizations, ICA was headed by more than one bank; member committees were created to run the association. They established rules for authorization, clearing, and settlement. They also handled marketing, security, and legal aspects of running the organization.

The organization began to expand globally, as soon as it gained firm footing within its region. In 1968, ICA began what is now a global network by forming an association with Banco Nacional in Mexico. Later that year, they formed an alliance in Europe with Eurocard. The first Japanese members also joined that year.

By the late 1970s, ICA had members from as far as Africa and Australia, among other places, with more than 5,000 financial institutions serving about 36 million of their own cards.

In 1969, the name was changed to Master Charge, and the logo design was updated to increase brand recognition. The graphic image was based on the two overlapping circles with the Master Charge title overlaid in the center of the logo. The symbol "i" stayed, but was significantly reduced, thus referencing the previous logo design.

To reflect its commitment to international growth, in 1979, ICA changed its name to MasterCard International and the symbol "i" disappeared from the logo.

In 1980, the number of MasterCard cards circulating in the US increased to 55 million, and by the end of 1990 this number reached 90 million. Between 1980 and 1991, the total volume of purchases through MasterCard system grew from 10.4 billion to almost 99 billion dollars.

In 1981 MasterCard introduced the first gold bank card program, and in 1983 MasterCard becomes the first to use the laser hologram as an antifraud device.

Further expansion of MasterCard in Asia and Latin America continued during the 1980s. In 1987, MasterCard card becomes the first payment card issued in the People's Republic of China, and a year later, in 1988, MasterCard entered into the Soviet Union

In 1989 MasterCard introduced the first bank card with a tamper-resistant signature panel. In 1990, MasterCard unveiled a co-branding strategy and became the industry's co-branding leader; the intersection of the double circle logo changed into 23 horizontal stripes. The redesign saw the

adoption of a more contemporary typeface and brighter colors.

In 1991, MasterCard, in partnership with Europay International, launched Maestro, the world's first truly global online debit program. In 1992, Maestro completed the first-ever coast-to-coast national online debit transaction in the United States. In the same year, EuroCard International merged with the EuroCheck payment system. The new organization was called Europay International. This new European card payment system started operating MasterCard International alongside the merger brands.

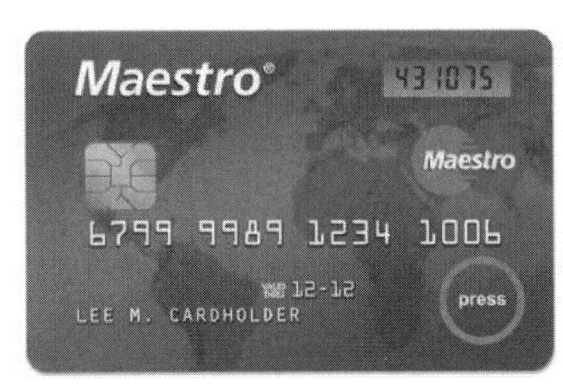

In 1994, MasterCard International began the development of a global chip specification for payment systems, two years later the EMV standard emerged, and in October 1997 MasterCard first plastic cards of this new standard were released in the UK.

According to the representatives of MasterCard Int, chip technologies have a number of advantages over magnetic stripe: they allow increasing the level of security in transactions, thereby reducing the likelihood of fraud, as well as reducing operating costs and promoting the development of new technologies, particularly, mobile commerce.

In 1996 MasterCard Global Service became the first program to provide cardholders with telephone access to core emergency and special services in 21 languages, from 130 countries (and today in 196 countries and 46 languages), and as part of a global effort to strengthen the MasterCard brand, a new, enhanced brand mark was unveiled. In the same year, MasterCard contract AT&T to replace its transaction network with the industry's first virtual private network design, which delivers faster response time and lower costs.

In 1997, MasterCard became the first payment system to set the unauthorized use limit of $50 for all credit and debit MasterCard cards issued in the US. At the same time, the company acquired a 51% stake in Mondex International.

In 1998 MasterCard/Cirrus ATM Network expanded to Antarctica, and MasterCard and MYCAL Card Company in Japan announced the world's first migration from traditional credit cards to multi-application chip cards using the MULTOS operating system.

In 1999 Mondex e-cash and MULTOS became the first commercial products ever to receive the highest assurance level possible under the prestigious ITSEC (Information Technology Security Evaluation Criteria) security rating. The first online purchase of a U.S. Treasury Bond was made with a MasterCard card.

MasterCard became the first in the industry to establish a U.S. rule of no liability for the consumer from the unauthorized use of payment cards.

In 2001, MasterCard launches mc² Card, the first non-rectangular card. It has the lower-right corner missing.

MasterCard becomes the first payments association to actively support all smart card platforms, enabling members to issue MasterCard, Maestro and Cirrus branded smart cards on MULTOS, JavaCard, or proprietary platforms.

In 2002, Europay International merged with MasterCard International. The name Europay disappeared, and the new organisation was later renamed MasterCard Worldwide. The merged entity became known as MasterCard Europe headquartered in Waterloo, Belgium.

Eurocard (absorbed by Europay in 1992) has always been the dominant brand in Central European countries, more specifically in Germany, Netherlands and Austria, but it lagged behind Visa in Southern European countries, such as Spain and France. Successful merger of MasterCard and Europay significantly improved the positions of MasterCard in the world and allowed the brand to compete with Visa International.

1.4. Types of Cards

Bank card is typically a plastic card associated with one or more of operating bank accounts.

VISA and MasterCard have three types of pay cards: debit, credit and stored-value cards.

Debit cards

A debit card can be used instead of cash when making purchases. It is similar to a credit card, but unlike a credit card, the money comes directly from the user's bank account when performing a transaction, within preset daily limit

In the case of debit card, there is no need in thorough verification of cardholder's identity or examining his credit history, which simplifies the card issuing process and reduces servicing costs. The balance of funds on the debit card account is sometimes subject to accrued interest, just as on an ordinary bank deposit.

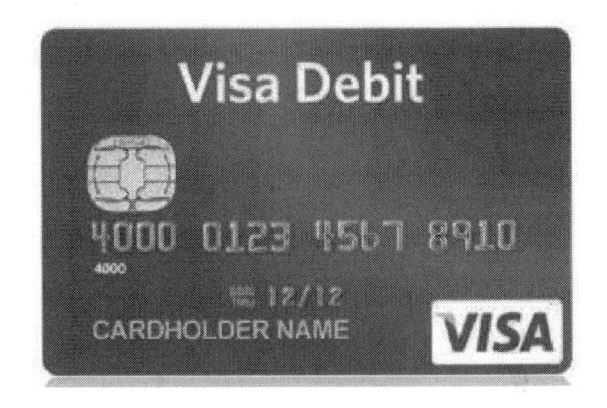

Charge cards

Though the terms charge card and credit card are sometimes used interchangeably, they are distinct protocols of financial transactions.

Charge cards is a card that provides a payment method enabling the cardholder to make purchases which are paid for by the card issuer, to whom the cardholder becomes indebted. A charge card requires the cardholder to pay off his balance in full each month. It doesn't have a preset limit. Instead, purchases are approved based on cardholder's spending and payment history, financial resources and credit record. Charge cards draw both on client's account and on a credit limit presented to the client by the bank. As long as there is money on hand for a purchase with a charge card, transactions draw on the available funds, but as soon as cardholder's funds become insufficient, the bank starts lending its client within established credit limit. Like credit cards, charge cards extend credit to the cardholder from the issuer, but he is required to pay the full balance at the end of the period specified in the contract.

The big advantage charge cards have over debit cards is that cardholder doesn't run the risk of overdraft fees, as is the case with debit cards. In the case of charge card, a cardholder is paying with own funds at hand just like a debit card, saving on loan interest, but has the option to borrow from the bank when short on funds.

Credit cards

A credit card, stated simply, is a form of loan: the bank or credit card issuer extends the cardholder a line of credit within a given limit according to the terms of the credit. The bank sets this limit according to the client's capacity to repay the credit. The balance of the credit card account accrues interest as well, however, it is usually far lower than the commission for overdraft.

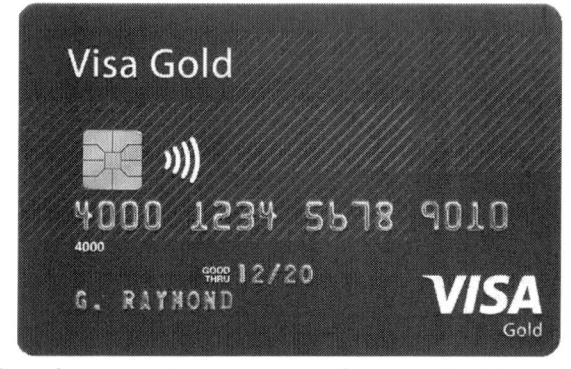

Banking products and services are frequently combined (card and credit), so it is rather difficult to unambiguously decide whether a credit card is a lending or a transactions tool. The main advantage of credit cards over loans is that a cardholder can borrow money from bank without reporting on its intended use, and permanently renew his credit line after repaying the debt. Typically, credit cards involve extended credit lines that are reimbursed in equal installments, which automatically renews the credit line. The difference between credit cards and charge cards is the absence of positive balance on the card. A credit card may assume both the presence of a loan from the bank or its absence. Even when the customer contributes an amount that exceeds the amount of debt, it is added to a separate account and is used only to pay off the next debt. Notable, a loan is reimbursed at a certain date fixed by the contract, and not immediately after it occurred. In some cases this is not really beneficial to the client, but a grace period often compensates for that.

Early Diners Club payment cards were credit cards that were meant to pay off on credit in restaurants, and then repay the loan at the end of the settlement period.

Prepaid Cards

A prepaid debit card is an alternative banking card that only lets a cardholder to spend the money he had loaded onto the card. Like a debit card, a prepaid card works at any merchant that accepts its payment network, such as Visa or MasterCard. It's safer and more convenient than using cash. It's also known as a pay-as-you-go card or, more formally, a general-purpose reloadable prepaid card.

In addition, there are a few dozen more narrow types of VISA and MasterCard.

Entry-level debit card

These include Visa Electron, VISA Electron Instant Issue, MasterCard Electronic, MasterCard Instant Issue and Maestro. The annual cost of maintenance is low for these cards, and they are used only in ATMs and POS terminals. They do not allow overspending. When using prepaid a card real time authorization is mandatory. Such cards are often issued by banks as payroll cards is arranged by an employer for the purpose of paying its employees' wages or salary; they are offered within retail lending programs, and offered free of charge in addition to other banking products, such as deposits. Such cards are called unembossed, because they do not carry raised lettering and hence can not be used with an imprinting machine. Moreover, Instant Issue cards are not personalized with owner's name.

Classic cards

VISA Classic and MasterCard Standard cards. These can be both credit and debit cards that are issued to people with stable income, and have an optimal ratio of servicing costs to services provided by the bank and payment system. These cards are "embossed" with owner's personal data and card's validity period. Embossed cards fit in standard credit card imprinters that read the card data. These cards allow offline and online payment for goods and services, withdrawing cash in ATMs and in different financial institutions worldwide. Classic or Standard cardholders are provided with emergency cash withdrawal or temporary card issuance service in case of loss.

Premium Cards

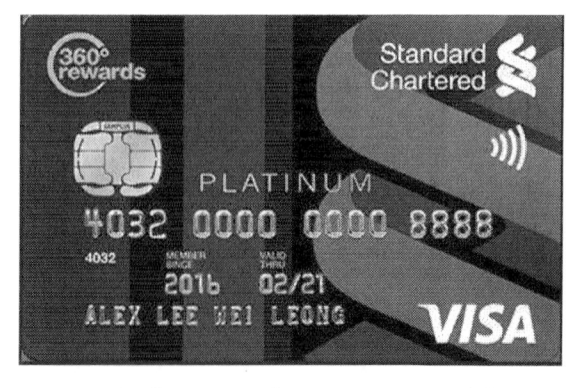

Credit and debit cards of Gold and Platinum level, as well as VISA Infinite and MasterCard World Signia cards belong in this group. In addition to the basic payment functions, these cards provide holders with a number of additional services. Each type of premium card has its own options offered by the payment system. Holders of gold cards are provided with information services. When traveling, they are advised on visa regulations in particular country, hospitals to be contacted in case of need, etc. Various insurance programs may be offered by the banks, as well as privileges, such as discounts in restaurants, boutiques, for hotel bookings, car rental, etc.

List of sources used

- Dee Hock "One from Many: VISA and the Rise of Chaordic Organization"

Self-control questions

1. Who founded the Visa payment system and what was it called initially?
2. What were the main reasons for renaming BankAmericard to Visa?
3. What was the MasterCard payment system originally called?
4. What company did MasterCard merge with that significantly strengthened its global standing?
5. How wold you define the concept of 'bank card'?
6. What are the three main types of Visa and MasterCard cards?
7. What is a debit card?
8. What is a credit card?
9. What is a prepaid card?
10. What Classic Visa and MasterCard cards do you know?
11. What Premium Visa and MasterCard cards do you know?
12. What is the main difference between Premium and Classic cards?

2. Settlement Participants

2.1. Basic concepts

A payment system is to be understood as a set of rules and means allowing settlements between the following parties: the buyer of a product or service, the commercial organization, and the financial institution that issued the card to its client enabling him to perform such transactions.

In Russia, the right to issue pay cards is limited to financial institutions that have an appropriate license from the Central Bank of Russia. In other countries, other institutions may be issuing payment cards as well, if permitted by the law, for example, Diners Club, or Principal and Associate members of Visa.

Banks, that are part of the so-called payment associations, occupy a special place among issuers of payment cards. In this part we will be mainly discussing them.

To begin with, let us recall some basic definitions:

- **Issuing Bank** is a financial institution, and a member of a payment system, that issues and services bank cards. It is assuming the role of a credit provider, warranting the fulfillment of financial obligations arising in the course of using the cards by holders. A bank card issued by a bank remains its property for the entire validity term, granting a cardholder the right for its use.
- **Financial institution** (FI) is a company engaged in the business of dealing with financial and monetary transactions, such as deposits, loans, investments and currency exchange. Financial institutions encompass a broad range of business operations within the financial services sector, including banks, trust companies, insurance companies, brokerage firms and investment dealers.
- **Acquiring bank** (also referred to as acquirer) is a financial institution that provides terminals and ATMs that accept cards, and manages the financial transactions related to settlements and payments by bank cards

wherever accepted.
- **Retail business establishment**, or Merchant, provides merchant services, i. e. authorized financial services that allow a business to accept credit or debit card transactions using online ordering or point of sales systems.
- **Acquiring** is the process of accepting payment cards for payment. The following types of acquiring are distinguished::
    - *ATM (Automated Teller Machine) acquiring* – accepting payment cards for cash delivery at ATM;
    - *Trade Point of Sale (POS) acquiring* – accepting payment cards for settlement of goods and services at retail business establishment using POS terminals;
    - *Internet-acquiring* – accepting payment cards for settlement of goods and services at online stores.

The principal task of Payment Systems is to create and operate system of mutual exchange. This is their key function and is in fact characteristic of a payment system. **Interchange** is an aggregate of transactions conducted within a system, performing authorization, mutual settlement and transfer of payments, as well as other financial and non-financial information exchange within Bank Card industry.

First, let us consider the **authorization** process:

Suppose a cardholder is at a restaurant and having lunch. He then decides to pay for it with his bank card. The waiter authorizes the transaction, i.e. transfers information about the card number and the amount of payment to the Acquirer. Additionally, this data includes the date and time of the transaction, as well as the account code of the Merchant.

In this example, for the sake of clarity, we will disregard the exact manner of doing it (it can be voice authorization through communication with the bank by phone, or using POS device that sends this information automatically). A cashier or seller (the waiter in this example) only the payment amount, and the card data is read by the device itself. The important thing is that this information is accepted by the Acquirer.

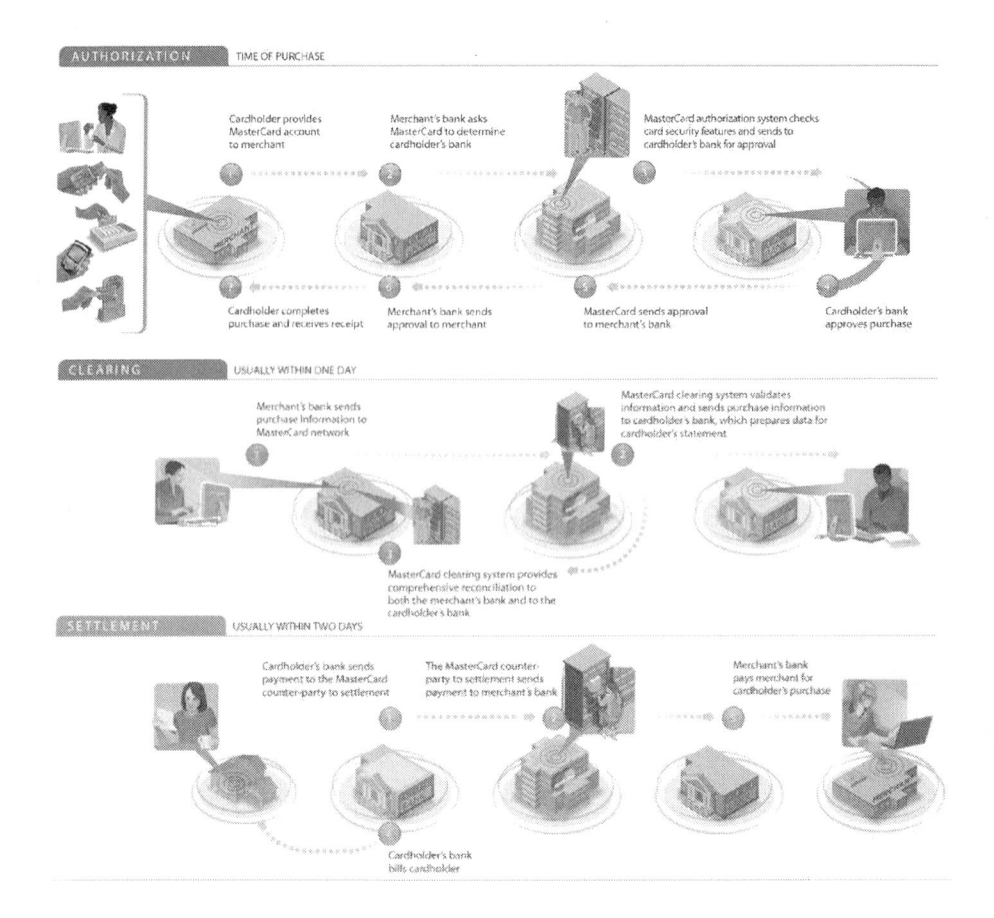

Then the Acquirer forwards this information to the payment system. The payment system transfers this data to the Issuer to check the customer's account. If such payment is possible, the corresponding amount is reserved by the Issuer, and a permission to conduct the transaction is sent back to the Acquirer. Having received the permission, the Acquirer sends informs its decision to Merchant organization. If authorization is declined, this means that the transaction was not approved, and the Merchant can not accept the given card for payment.

This is how it works in general. Obviously, a payment authorization process is much more complex, and technically a payment data can be processed by a number of agents. Moreover, a payment system allocates risks in such a way that an approval for a transaction can be obtained without querying the issuer.

It should be noted that historically there used to be 'floor limits'[7] at each stage of a transaction, below which its approval occurred automatically. For example, a payment terminal may not query the Acquirer (or, more precisely, the computer located at the Acquirer's premises or at the processing company). In case the amount of payment is less than the limit set by the Acquirer, the terminal itself will issue a permit for the transaction, and simply print a sales receipt.

These days, voice authorization, a request to a human operator for authorization, is now occasionally used only at the Merchant-to-Acquirer stage of transaction, with the rest of the data going through automatic processing.

What happens when our waiter receives an authorization code? Within this transaction a debtor-creditor relationship arises between the system participants. Who owes money to the Merchant organization? Acquirer does. Who owes money to the Acquirer? The system does (or, more precisely, the settlement bank). Who owes money to the system? The Issuer does. Who owes money to the issuer? The Cardholder who had lunch at the restaurant does. No cash flows did occur, and the restaurant at this stage has so far received only an authorization code but not money.

Such relations are established for each transaction. The payment system starts to resolve these relations immediately after a payment takes place. The issuer transfers the reserved amount of the authorized transaction to the settlement bank, the settlement bank transfers it to the Acquirer and finally, the Acquirer transfers the money to the Merchant's account.

Again, the calculation principle here is outlined in general terms. The settlement of debt process can take longer. Acquirer and issuer can be the same entity. In this case, as an Acquirer, it communicates to the payment system all claims for reimbursement of transaction amounts for all the cards that are "alien" to it. Whereas the transactions with its own cards are settled on-the-spot if internal processing is available. Meanwhile, the Acquirer receives funds from the system as an Issuer, responding to requests for transactions carried out with its clients' cards in the commercial networks of other acquirers, with due offset for its interests as an Acquirer.

The **Clearing** process is the totality of procedures that start with authorization and end with the transfer of funds from the issuing bank to the acquiring bank (or rather, to the Merchant's account in the acquiring bank).

In fact, the exact mode of settling the "debtor-creditor" relation within the payment system is not that important. The key point is that all the amounts on authorized transactions should be received from the Acquirer in time and in full. The Acquirer in turn receives its service commission from the Merchant.

This way, the transaction process consists of two main phases: one is **authorization**, the other is **clearing and settlement**.

Authorization is the process of obtaining permission from the issuing bank to accept the card for payment. **Clearing and settlement** is the process of sending a transaction through the PSP of Visa or MasterCard to a Merchant.

The authorization starts the moment the card data is transferred to the Payment Service Provider for payment. Normally, authorization is performed at the point-of-sale terminal, however, a raising number of transactions is being carried out in card absent environment (for online payment, for example). PSPs receive the authorization date in electronic form from POS terminal, which either reads it automatically, or alternatively it can be entered manually.

Once the authorization is completed, clearing and settlement process begins. When a consumer buys something with his payment card, contractual obligations between him and a Merchant emerge. The Merchant agrees to deliver goods or provide services, and the consumer agrees to pay for it. Settlements is a process of implementing mutual commitments by transferring relevant assets. The Clearing process is a chain of transactions starting at the time of purchase and ending according to the results of the mutual settlement. Typically, clearing involves the transfer of data, but not assets. The most common example of clearing in payment card industry is the process of transferring transaction data from merchant to its acquiring bank. Hence, clearing includes transactions that provide mutual settlement. Simply put, authorization initiates a transaction reserving money on cardholder's account, then

3.3.3. Acquirer

1.5.1.1 Acquirer Jurisdiction and Restriction of Cross-Border Acquiring

An Acquirer must accept and submit Transactions into Interchange only from Payment Facilitators, Merchants, and Sponsored Merchants within that Acquirer's jurisdiction.

An Acquirer must accept Transactions only from a Merchant Outlet within the Acquirer's licensed Country of Domicile unless any of the following:

- The Acquirer is licensed to accept Transactions from a Merchant Outlet in another country.
- The Merchant is an International Airline and the Acquirer maintains the relationship in accordance with the provisions of the International Airline Program.[11]
- The Merchant Outlet is, or is located in or on the premises of, a military base, embassy, or consulate or international governmental organization (for example: the United Nations) on foreign territory.

A Payment Facilitator must not contract with a Sponsored Merchant that is outside the country in which the Payment Facilitator and its Acquirer are located unless either:

- The Sponsored Merchant is an International Airline and the Acquirer and Payment Facilitator maintain the relationship as specified in the Visa Rules regarding provisions of the International Airline Program.
- The Sponsored Merchant is a military base, embassy, or consulate on foreign territory. Visa considers these Sponsored Merchants to be within the Acquirer's Country and Region of Domicile

Exceptions to these rules apply to the United States and Canada. A Canada or US Acquirer may cross-border acquire Electronic Commerce Transactions.

1.5.1.2 Merchant Qualification Standards

Before entering into a Merchant Agreement, an Acquirer must ensure that the prospective Merchant is all of the following:

clearing completes this transaction, eventually transferring the funds to where they are due.

Visa and MasterCard payment systems have an Operating Center to process authorization, a payment clearing center to perform clearing, while mutual settlements go through a settlement center.

The **Operating Center** is an organization providing access to money transfer services for payment system's participants and their clients, as well as performing electronic messaging (hereinafter, operating services).

At this time Visa has four operating centers scattered around the world: two of them are in the US, one in the UK and one in Japan. The exchange of messages between the participants of the system is carried out through VisaNet.

VisaNet is the computer and telecommunications network which links over 19,000 of Visa's member financial institutions worldwide with the two Visa Interchange Centres and with each other. Two applications are managed through VisaNet:

- **Base I** authorization service;
- **Base II** clearing and settlement service.

Mastercard operates **Banknet**, a global telecommunications network linking all Mastercard card issuers, acquirers, and data processing centers into a single financial network. The operations hub is located in St. Louis, Missouri.

Mastercard's network differs significantly from Visa's. Visa's is a star-based system where all endpoints terminate at one of several main data centers, where all transactions are processed centrally. Mastercard's network is an edge-based, peer-to-peer network[8] where transactions travel a meshed network directly to other endpoints, without the need to travel to a single point. This allows Mastercard's network to be much more resilient, in that a single failure cannot isolate a large number of endpoints.

In Russia As postulated in the Federal Law of June 27, 2011, No. 161-FZ "On the National Payment System" (as amended by Federal Law No. 112-FZ of 05.05.2014), money transfer service providers should exclusively contract providers with the entirety of their functions performed within the territory of the Russian

Federation. In other words, the operation and clearing centers should necessarily be located on the territory of Russia. Hence, in Russia, Visa and MasterCard are operated by the National Payment Card System (AO NSPK).

PSD2 contains an option for EU Member States to require a payment institution that provides cross-border payment services to set up a central contact point if it operates with agents or branches that are established in their territory. The central contact point shall ensure adequate communication and information with regard to the activities of the payment institution in the host territory. The European Banking Authority is mandated to draft regulatory technical standards on the criteria under which a central contact point can be requested, and the functions of such contact point.

Payment Clearing House is a common entity (or a common processing mechanism) through which participants agree to exchange transfer instructions for funds. The role of the clearing house is to centralize and standardize all of the steps leading up to the payment (i.e. settlement) of the transaction. The cycle of processing input data (clearing files) is called **clearing cycle**. After completing the cycle, the clearing center gives instructions to the settlement center to conduct settlement transactions. AO NSPK is also operating the clearing center.

A **Settlement Center** is an organization that executes the instructions of payment system participants by means of debiting and crediting funds on the accounts of participants in the payment system, as well as by sending confirmations for such operations (hereinafter, settlement services). Since March 5, 2015, in Russia, the Settlement Center of Visa and MasterCard is the Central Bank of Russia. Prior to that, VTB and Sberbank assumed the functions of the Settlement Center.

The clearing cycle in the NSPK starts at 9:00 AM Moscow time and lasts 24 hours. The cycle is repeated daily. Settlements on accounts of participants occur one day after the transaction is closed. The Bank of Russia performs settlements at participants accounts on Bank of Russia payment system's operating days, from 11:00 to 21:00 Moscow time. For each payment system, settlements are performed by a separate order to participant's correspondent account in the Bank of Russia. If the settlement date falls on a weekend or a holiday, its processing is resumed on the next business day and recorded by the same order to participant's correspondent account in the Bank of Russia. In other words, in Russia, the acquiring bank actually receives money from the payment system only on the third day.

Self-control questions

1. Give a definition for the Issuing Bank.
2. Define the concept of the Acquiring Bank.
3. What types of acquiring do you know?
4. What is the main function of a payment system?
5. What are the two phases of a transaction?
6. Describe the authorization process.
7. What is floor limit?
8. What does "clearing" stand for?
9. What is Operating Center and what does it do?
10. What are VisaNet, Base1 and Base2?
11. Name the equivalent of VisaNet for MasterCard. What is their essential difference?
12. What is the difference between Clearing and Operating centers?
13. How soon does Acquiring Bank receive funds from the Payment System?

3. The Rules of Payment Systems

This section contains extracts and explanations from Visa Public Rules. These extracts and explanations refer to the general requirements for the participants of the payment system and merchants in the field of electronic commerce. The description does not claim to be complete and does not cover all the variety of issues. The rules relating to High-Risk business are described in the relevant section along with the risks.

We will recapitulate the basic definitions to begin with.

3.1. Definitions

Issuer is a financial organization, a participant in the payment system, which issues and services bank cards. It guarantees the fulfillment of financial obligations that arise in the course of using these cards by their holders. A bank card issued by a bank remains its property for the entire validity term, granting a cardholder the right for its use.

Acquirer is a financial institution that provides terminals and ATMs that accept cards, and manages the financial transactions related to settlements and payments by bank cards wherever accepted.

Merchant is a retail business establishment, an organization that accepts bank cards for payment for goods and services.

Merchant Account is a type of bank account that allows businesses to accept payments in multiple ways, typically debit or credit cards.

Payment Facilitator is an agent (a third party) that can:
- sign agreements with merchants on behalf of Acquirer;
- receive reimbursement for processed transactions from Acquirer on behalf of Sponsored Merchant.

Sponsored Merchant is a merchant to which payment services are provided by Payment Facilitator.

Primary Account Number (PAN) is simply the card number. Each bank card has a unique number. The number on the card can be printed or embossed.

The card number is governed by two standards:

- the international standard ISO/IEC 7812-1 (issued by SWIFT);
- GOST R 50809-95 (issued by the Association of Engineering and Automation Centers (St. Petersburg).

Current international standard specifies the following structure for the identification number of a plastic card:

BBBBBBNNNNNNNNNNNNL, where BBBBBB is the issuer's identification number (BIN);

NNNNNNNNNNNN – the identification number of a plastic card itself, its length may be 7, 10 or 13 digits;

L – a single check digit calculated using the Luhn algorithm (a checksum formula used to validate the previous digits of the number) is optional and can be found only on cards with a 13-digit number.

Normally, payment cards have only 16 digits (four groups of four digits, the first six are BIN), old cards can have 13 (the first group of four digits and three groups of three digits, are among the very old programs open for individual regions). There are cards with 18 and 19 digits, as a rule, the first 16 digits are used as usual, and the rest (except for the L digit) define a subroutine or issuer's sub-division.

Bank Identification Number (BIN) is a bank identification number. BIN is present on any bank card, it is represented in the first 6 digits on its front side. BIN serves for identification of a bank in payment systems for transactions with a card. For example, if the first digit of a card number is 4, then it refers to the Visa system. Other systems can also be uniquely identified by the first two or three digits of BIN, but the algorithm for identifying them is more complex. From a BIN number you can find out the type of your card (credit or debit), figure out a premium level of a card (Electron, Classic, Gold, etc.), find out the country and the organization that issued the card.

Processing Date in MMDDYYYY format is the date an acquiring bank processed a card transaction that was authorized by a merchant.

Processing is a general term describing the multi-step process of transferring funds from Cardholder to Merchant. Processing date is the date the interbank clearing and settlement takes place.

Transaction Date is the date the transaction was authorized.

3.2. Merchant registration with IPS

3.2.1. MID, TID, GID

Merchant Identification Number (MID) is a unique number assigned to a Merchant Account for identification within the entire payment processing processes.

When a Merchant is processing a card transaction through a computer network, such a network is connected to the operational and clearing centers of the IPS through a network gateway. A Merchant Account contains the Merchant Identification Number (MID), one or more **Terminal Identification Numbers (TID)**, and a **Gateway Identification Number (GID)**. The MID uniquely identifies a merchant as a legal entity, whereas the TID points to a particular point of sale, a location or a facility from which the transactions is initiated. The GID identifies a particular network gateway through which card transactions are routed to the operational and clearing centers.

MID is generated by Processor or by Acquirer and is specific to each Merchant as a legal entity (for this purpose a Merchant can simultaneously have multiple MIDs). This number is used to identify a Merchant when processing transactions, adjustments, chargebacks, end of month fees, etc. It is very important not to confuse the MID with other Merchant Account numbers, in particular, those that identify the equipment for processing transactions. A Merchant with a single MID number can have several terminals in one location, resulting in a single MID and multiple TIDs.

MIDs assigned to different points of sale of your company identify them as separate accounting entities, which allows you to identify data for each point of sale in the reports.

...m describing the multi-step process ... Cardholder to Merchant. Processing ...rbank clearing and settlement takes

... is the date the transaction was authorized.

...t registration with IPS

3.2... ..D, TID, GID

Merchant Identification Number (MID) is a unique number assigned to a Merchant Account for identification within the entire payment processing processes.

When a Merchant is processing a card transaction through a computer network, such a network is connected to the operational and clearing centers of the IPS through a network gateway. A Merchant Account contains the Merchant Identification Number (MID), one or more **Terminal Identification Numbers (TID)**, and a **Gateway Identification Number (GID)**. The MID uniquely identifies a merchant as a legal entity, whereas the TID points to a particular point of sale, a location or a facility from which the transactions is initiated. The GID identifies a particular network gateway through which card transactions are routed to the operational and clearing centers.

MID is generated by Processor or by Acquirer and is specific to each Merchant as a legal entity (for this purpose a Merchant can simultaneously have multiple MIDs). This number is used to identify a Merchant when processing transactions, adjustments, chargebacks, end of month fees, etc. It is very important not to confuse the MID with other Merchant Account numbers, in particular, those that identify the equipment for processing transactions. A Merchant with a single MID number can have several terminals in one location, resulting in a single MID and multiple TIDs.

MIDs assigned to different points of sale of your company identify them as separate accounting entities, which allows you to identify data for each point of sale in the reports.

3.2.2. MCC

Merchant Category Code (MCC) MCC is a four-digit number and is used in the banking card industry for the classification of merchants according to the type of their activity.

MCC code is assigned by the acquiring bank to a Merchant in order to accept cards. Such a code is appointed according to Merchant's primary area of business activity, and should accurately characterize the essence of the services provided. For example, if an outlet is primarily engaged in the sale of computers, then it may be assigned the code 5732 (Electronics Stores), if it is engaged in computer repair and servicing, then the code should be 7379 (Computer Repair).

3.2.3. Descriptor

Descriptor is what your customers will see on their statement when they order goods in your store. Ultimately, the buyer's bank will exactly determine the descriptors of your business to appear on the buyers' statement. Normally descriptors are formatted as follows:

MYCOMPANYNAME 555-123-1234

Depending on the acquirer and the underlying technology used to process transactions, it will be either possible or impossible to specify a handle for each individual transaction. The term "dynamic descriptor" is used to indicate that the underlying system is able to describe transactions at each transactional level during processing, and as a result, each transaction will receive its own descriptor. When the term "static descriptor" is used, it is understood that a descriptor for all transactions processed through this MID is specified at the level of the entire MID, and therefore a description of individual transactions is impossible to extract.

3.2.4. Registration

When registering a Merchant Account in the MAP, the Acquirer assigns one or more MIDs to a retail and service outlet, depending on the types of goods and services its business activity is made up of. Each MID is assigned its own MCC. For each MID one or more TID is created (i.g., individual TID codes for each of the cash desks inside a supermarket). For example, when one retail and service outlet is selling gasoline and carbonated water at a gas station, then this TSP will have at least two MID codes assigned to it with different MCCs.

3.3. Visa Public Rules

For more information, please refer to the source:

https://usa.visa.com/dam/VCOM/download/about-visa/visa-rules-public.pdf

Visa Core Rules contain basic guidelines for all Visa members and set minimum requirements for all participants, providing or the safety, security, stability, integrity and compatibility of the Visa system.

Visa Product and Service Rules contain rules applicable to all users and participants of products, services, Visa trademarks, VisaNet, dispute resolution process, and other aspects of the Visa payment system. Visa Product and Service Rules also include operational requirements concerning Visa Core Rules.

3.3.1. General Provisions

1.1.1.2 Applicable Laws and Conflicts

A Transaction must be legal in both the Cardholder's jurisdiction and the Merchant Outlet's jurisdiction. In the event of any conflict between the Visa Rules and any applicable laws or regulations, the requirements of the laws or regulations govern.

1.1.1.6 Visa Inc. Regions and Visa Europe Territory

Visa assigns all countries of countries world into 6 regions[9]:

- Asia-Pacific Region
- Canada Region
- Central and Eastern Europe, Middle East and Africa Region (Visa CEMEA)
- Latin America and Caribbean Region (LAC Region)
- US Region

- Visa Europe Territory (Visa Europe)

1.1.6.1 Visa Ownership of Intellectual Property

A participant in the Visa system must recognize Visa's ownership of its intellectual property, including the Visa name, Visa Marks, and Visa technology, and agree to protect these ownership rights and the integrity of the Marks by complying with the applicable Visa Rules in all activities, including issuing, acquiring, and processing.

1.1.6.2 Visa Right to Monitor, Audit, Inspect, and Investigate

At its sole discretion, at any time, Visa may, either itself or through an agent, do any of the following:

- Investigate, review, audit, or inspect a Member, or the Member's agents, Merchants, Sponsored Merchants, or Payment Facilitators, including by inspecting the premises and auditing the books, records, and procedures of the Member, agent, Merchant, Sponsored Merchant, or Payment Facilitator to ensure that it is complying with the Visa Rules and applicable brand and security standards and procedures.
- Monitor, investigate, review, audit, or inspect the premises, books, records, or procedures of an Approved Manufacturer or Third-Party Personalizer, including security and quality control procedures of each Approved Manufacturer and Third-Party Personalizer
- Obtain from any Approved Manufacturer or Third-Party Personalizer a production-run sample of a Visa Card that includes all security features

A Member must cooperate fully, and ensure that its agent, Merchant, Sponsored Merchant, or Payment Facilitator cooperates fully, with Visa in any such investigation, inspection, audit, or review. This cooperation includes providing access to the premises and to all pertinent records and releasing any information to Visa upon request. Any investigation, inspection, review, or audit will be conducted at the Member's expense, unless otherwise specified in the applicable Fee Schedule.

3.3.2. Issuer

1.4.3 Notification and Disclosure

1.4.3.1 Notification of Card Use Restrictions

An Issuer must include language in its Cardholder agreement that a Card must not be used for any unlawful purpose, including the purchase of goods or services prohibited by applicable laws or regulations.

1.4.3.2 International Transaction or Currency Conversion Fee Disclosure

An Issuer must provide a complete written disclosure of any fees that may be charged to a Cardholder for an International Transaction or when currency conversion occurs.

1.4.3.3 Recurring Transaction Data on Cardholder Billing Statement

An Issuer must include on the Cardholder billing statement the data transmitted in the Clearing Record that both:

- Identifies a Recurring Services Merchant
- Enables the Cardholder to contact the Merchant

1.4.3.4 Cardholder Signature on Card

When an Issuer issues or reissues a Card, the Issuer must:

- Advise the Cardholder to immediately sign the signature panel on the Card
- Indicate that the Card must be signed in order to be valid

1.7.4.2 Decline Response Prohibition for Electronic Commerce Transactions

An Issuer must not systematically send a Decline Response to an Authorization Request for an Electronic Commerce Transaction coded with Electronic Commerce Indicator 6 unless there is an immediate fraud threat.

This prohibition does not apply to Visa Cards issued with restrictions that are clearly communicated to the Cardholder.

Visa controls the level of refusals provided by the Issuer

on transactions with the e-commerce indicator set to value 6. An Issuer is deemed to be non-compliant if it exceeds 500 Authorizations a month and a decline rate of 50% or more for Transactions containing Electronic Commerce Indicator 6.

7.3.4 Member Provision of Authorization Services

7.3.4.1 Authorization Service Requirement

A Member must provide Authorization services for all of its Cardholders or Merchants, 24 hours a day, 7 days a week, using one of the following methods:

- Directly, as a VisaNet Processor
- Through another VisaNet Processor, including Visa
- By other means approved by Visa

7.3.4.2 Issuer Authorization Response Requirements

An Issuer must provide Authorization Responses and all of the following:

- Meet the assured Transaction response standards
- Participate in the International Automated Referral Service[10].
- Participate in the Card Verification Service

7.3.5 Authorization Request Time Limits

7.3.5.1 Intraregional Authorization Requests – Maximum Time Limit for Response.

The maximum time limit for a response to an Authorization Request for an Intraregional Transaction is:

- 15 seconds without PIN data
- 30 seconds with PIN data
- In the CEMEA Region, 25 seconds with PIN data

If Visa does not receive an Authorization Response from an Issuer within the specified time limit, Visa will respond on behalf of the Issuer, using Stand-In Processing.

- Financially responsible
- Not engaged in any activity that could cause harm to the Visa system or the Visa brand
- Operating within an allowed jurisdiction

The Acquirer and Payment Facilitator must also determine that there is no significant derogatory background information about any of the Merchant's principals.

1.5.1.3 Submission of Illegal Transactions

An Acquirer must not knowingly accept from a Merchant for submission into the Visa payment system any Transaction that is illegal or that the Acquirer or Merchant should have known was illegal.

1.5.1.7 Termination of Merchant Agreement

After verifying that Visa has prohibited a Merchant or Sponsored Merchant from participating in the Visa or Visa Electron Program, an Acquirer must terminate the Merchant Agreement no later than the date specified by Visa. If the Acquirer does not terminate the Merchant Agreement by the specified date, Visa may assess the Acquirer a non-compliance assessment.

An Acquirer or Payment Facilitator that enters into a Merchant Agreement with a Merchant, Sponsored Merchant, or known principals of a Merchant or Sponsored Merchant that Visa has prohibited from participating in the Visa Program or Visa Electron Program may be assessed a non-compliance assessment.

1.5.6 Card and Cardholder Verification Requirements

1.5.6.2 Electronic Commerce Data Protection

An Acquirer must ensure that its Electronic Commerce Merchant offers Cardholders a Data Protection Method, such as Verified by Visa or Secure Sockets Layer (SSL).

1.7 Transaction Processing

1.7.1 General Processing

1.7.1.1 Authorization, Clearing, and Settlement of International Transactions through VisaNet

A Visa participant must authorize, clear, and settle messages for international Visa Transactions through

VisaNet and report to Visa all domestic Visa Transactions processed outside of VisaNet.

In some jurisdictions, a participant must authorize, clear, and settle all Visa Transactions through VisaNet, which enhances Visa's ability to manage risks, meet consumer expectations, and provide leading fraud-protection solutions.

1.7.3 Acquirer Authorization Requests

1.7.3.2 Authorization Currency and Conversion

An Authorization Request must be expressed in USD or the Transaction Currency.

If the Transaction Currency is not USD, an Acquirer may convert the Authorization amount into USD before sending the Authorization Request to Visa. If the Acquirer converts the Authorization amount, it must use a generally accepted Currency Conversion Rate.

1.10 Risk

1.10.1 Corporate Risk Reduction

1.10.1.3 Visa Right to Terminate Merchants, Payment Facilitators, or Sponsored Merchants.

Visa may permanently prohibit a Merchant, Payment Facilitator, Sponsored Merchant, or any other entity, or one of its principals, from participating in the Visa Program or Visa Electron Program for any reasons it deems appropriate, such as:

- Fraudulent activity;
- Presenting Transaction Receipts that do not result from an act between a Cardholder and a Merchant or Sponsored Merchant (laundering);
- Entering into a Merchant Agreement or Payment Facilitator Agreement under a new name with the intent to circumvent the Visa Rules;
- Activity that causes the Acquirer to repeatedly violate the Visa Rules;
- Activity that has resulted in Visa prohibiting the Merchant, Sponsored Merchant, or Payment Facilitator from participating in the Visa Program or Visa Electron Program;

- Exceeding the Global Merchant Chargeback Monitoring Program thresholds;
- Any other activity that may result in undue economic hardship or damage to the goodwill of the Visa system.

Visa may contact a Merchant, a Sponsored Merchant, or a Payment Facilitator directly, if warranted.

1.10.1.4 Acquirer Responsibility for Costs Due to Failure to Terminate a Merchant

An Acquirer is responsible for all costs incurred by Visa due to the Acquirer's failure to terminate a Merchant, Sponsored Merchant, or Payment Facilitator. This includes attorney's fees and costs of any legal action undertaken by Visa to protect the goodwill of the Visa system or to prevent further harm to Members and Cardholders.

1.10.3 Investigations

1.10.3.1 Investigation Assistance to Other Members

A Member must assist other Members in an investigation of fraudulent activity with a Visa Card or Visa Electron Card by performing tasks including, but not limited to, the following:

- Interviewing Merchants, Sponsored Merchants, Cardholders, suspects, witnesses, and law enforcement personnel;
- Obtaining handwriting samples, photographs, fingerprints, and any other similar physical evidence;
- Recovering lost, stolen, or Counterfeit Cards;
- Providing information to proper authorities for the possible arrest of suspects, at the Issuer's request;
- Performing any other reasonable investigative assistance;
- Inspecting the facilities of credit card manufacturers, embossers, encoders, mailers, and chip embedders.

5.1 Responsibilities Related to Information and Notification

5.1.1 Provision of Information, Registration, and Reporting

5.1.1.1 Provision of Required Merchant Information (Updated)

In a Visa Region where the collection of Merchant data is required, an Acquirer or its Agent must provide to Visa the following information for each Merchant or Sponsored Merchant. The information must be accurate, updated whenever the information changes, and in the format specified by Visa.

- T/A (trading as) or DBA (doing business as) name
- Full legal name (if different from DBA name). For a sole proprietor, the information must include the sole proprietor's full first and last name, including the middle initial.
- Merchant Outlet address (including street address, city, state/province and postal code)
- Telephone number (not required for Sponsored Merchants)
- Acquirer-assigned Merchant ID
- Card acceptor identification
- Merchant business registration number or tax identification number
- Payment Facilitator name (for Sponsored Merchants only)

5.2 Acquirer Responsibilities Related to Merchants

5.2.1 Merchant Agreements, Merchant Onboarding, and Merchant Relationships

5.2.1.1 Requirements for Acquirers Soliciting Electronic Commerce Merchant Applications

An Acquirer soliciting Merchant applications must list Merchant domicile requirements on its website.

5.2.1.2 Due Diligence Review of Prospective Merchant or Sponsored Merchant.

Before contracting with a prospective Merchant, an Acquirer must conduct an appropriate examination to ensure that it complies with the obligation to submit only legal transactions to the VisaNet system.

5.2.1.10 Merchant Category Code Assignment

An Acquirer must assign to a Merchant Outlet the MCC that most accurately describes its business.

An Acquirer must assign 2 or more MCCs to a Merchant

Outlet if either:

- The Merchant Outlet has deployed an Automated Fuel Dispenser and sells fuel or other goods or services in a Face-to-Face Environment.
- Separate lines of business are located at the same Merchant Outlet and one or more of the following applies:
    - A separate Merchant Agreement exists for each line of business.
    - Multiple Merchant Outlets on the same premises display different Merchant names.
    - One of the lines of business is designated by Visa to be a High-Brand Risk Merchant.
    - An Electronic Commerce Merchant Outlet contains a link to a separate electronic commerce website, and each website qualifies for a different MCC.

5.2.1.11 Merchant Name Assignment

The name used to identify a Merchant must be all of the following:

- The name it primarily uses to identify itself to its customers
- Displayed at each Merchant Outlet or on an Electronic Commerce Merchant's website
- Used consistently, including spelling, in every place that it is used, including, but not limited to, the:
    - Transaction Receipt provided to the Cardholder
    - Authorization Request
    - Clearing Record
    - Chargeback and Representment records

The Acquirer must correct non-compliant Merchant names or those causing Cardholder confusion.

5.8.4.2 Prohibition against Split Transaction (Updated)

A Merchant must not split a transaction by using 2 or more Transaction Receipts, except for the following:

- Advance Deposit Transactions
- Delayed Delivery Transactions
- Individual Airline tickets
- Ancillary Purchase Transactions
- Individual Cruise Line tickets
- Installment Transactions

- A transaction in which part of the amount is paid with a Visa Card and the other part paid with another Visa Card or other form of payment.

5.9.3.3 Acquirer Support of Verified by Visa (Updated)

An Acquirer must comply with all of the following:

- Notify its Electronic Commerce Merchant of the availability of Verified by Visa.
- Provide Verified by Visa to its Electronic Commerce Merchant as requested.
- And, for CEMEA Region: Process Electronic Commerce Transactions using Verified by Visa

3.3.4. Merchant

1.5.2 Merchant Agreements

1.5.2.1 Merchant Agreement Requirements.

An Acquirer must have a Merchant Agreement with each of its Merchants to accept Visa Cards and, if applicable, Visa Electron Cards. A Payment Facilitator must have a Merchant Agreement with each of its Sponsored Merchants.

The Merchant Agreement must include language that requires the Merchant to do all of the following:

- Perform its obligations under the Merchant Agreement in compliance with applicable laws or regulations
- Comply with the Visa Rules regarding use of the Visa-Owned Marks, Visa acceptance, risk management, Transaction processing, and any Visa products, programs, or services in which the Merchant is required to, or chooses to, participate.
- Not knowingly submit any Transaction that is illegal or that the Merchant should have known was illegal
- Include the right of Visa to limit or terminate the Acquirer's agreement with the Merchant or the Payment Facilitator's agreement with the Sponsored Merchant.

An Acquirer and a Payment Facilitator may accept Transactions only from an entity with which it has a valid Merchant Agreement.

1.5.3 Marks Display

1.5.3.1 Display of Card Acceptance Marks.

A Member or Merchant must display the appropriate Visa-Owned Marks to indicate which Cards it accepts for payment except in the case of a Merchant that either:

- Does not deal with the general public (for example: a private club);
- Is prohibited by trade association rules.

1.5.5 Card Acceptance Prohibitions

1.5.5.1 Prohibition of Minimum or Maximum Transaction Amount

A Merchant must not establish a minimum or maximum Transaction amount as a condition for honoring a Visa Card or Visa Electron Card.

5.8.4.5 Merchant Submission of Authorization Reversals

A Merchant must submit an Authorization Reversal:

- For the Authorization amount, if the Transaction is not completed;
- For the difference between the final Transaction amount and the Authorization amount, if the final Transaction amount is less;
- For a Transaction initiated in a Card-Present Environment, within 24 hours of the original Authorization;
- For a Transaction initiated in a Card-Absent Environment, within either:
  - 72 hours of the original Authorization;
  - 7 calendar days of the original Authorization Request if the final Transaction amount is less than the authorized amount.
- For a Hotel, Car Rental Company, or Cruise Line Transaction, within 24 hours of the check-out, rental return, or disembarkation date;
- For a Transaction involving an estimated or incremental Authorization at a transit Merchant (MCC 4111, 4112, or 4131), within 24 hours of the final Authorization.

5.9.3 Electronic Commerce

5.9.3.1 Merchant Website Requirements

An Electronic Commerce Merchant Website must contain all of the following:

- Customer service contact, including email address or telephone number
- The address, including the country, of the Merchant's or Sponsored Merchant's Permanent Establishment,[12] either:
  - On the same screen view as the checkout screen used to present the final Transaction amount;
  - Within the sequence of web pages the Cardholder accesses during the checkout process.
- Policy for delivery of multiple shipments.
- Security capabilities and policy for transmission of payment card details.
- In addition, on an Online Gambling Merchant's homepage or payment page, all of the following:
  - The statement "Internet gambling may be illegal in the jurisdiction in which you are located; if so, you are not authorized to use your payment card to complete this transaction."
  - A statement of the Cardholder's responsibility to know the laws concerning online gambling in the Cardholder's country.
  - A statement prohibiting the participation of minors.
  - A complete description of the rules of play, cancellation policies, and pay-out policies.
  - A statement recommending that the Cardholder retain a copy of Transaction records and Merchant policies and rules.
  - An Acquirer numeric identifier specified by Visa.

5.9.3.2 Electronic Commerce Account Number Security

An Electronic Commerce Merchant must not display the full Account Number to the Cardholder online.

5.9.3.6 Online Gambling Merchant Requirements

An Online Gambling Merchant must both:

- Have a valid license or other appropriate authority to operate its website;
- Identify an Online Gambling Transaction with both:
  - MCC 7995 (Betting), even when gambling services are not the Merchant's primary business
  - The Quasi-Cash/Online Gambling Transaction indicator.

If a Member, Merchant, Payment Facilitator, or Sponsored Merchant is unable to distinguish an Online Gambling Transaction from other Transactions, it must both:

- Identify all Transactions as Online Gambling Transactions;
- Inform the Cardholder that Transactions may be identified on the billing statement as gambling Transactions.

5.9.3.8 Disbursement of Gambling Winnings to a Cardholder

A gambling Merchant must not deposit a credit Transaction to disburse gambling winnings to a Cardholder except for an Original Credit Transaction.

If a gambling Merchant uses an Original Credit Transaction to disburse gambling winnings to a Cardholder, it must ensure that both the:

- Original Credit Transaction is processed to the same Account Number that was used to place the winning wager.
- Transaction representing the winning wager was lawfully made, properly identified, and processed according to the Visa Rules.

5.9.4 Mail / Phone Order Transactions

5.9.4.1 Disclosure of Mail/Phone Order Merchant Outlet Country

A Mail/Telephone Order Merchant (MO/TO) must disclose the Merchant Outlet country when presenting payment options to a Cardholder.

5.9.8.2 Recurring Transaction Merchant Requirements (Updated)

For a Recurring Transaction, a Merchant must do all of the following:

- Obtain the Cardholder's legally recognized consent to periodically charge for recurring goods or services. This permission must include at least all of the following:
    - The Transaction amount, unless the Recurring Transactions are for varying amounts;
    - The frequency of the recurring charges;
    - The duration for which Cardholder permission is granted;
    - Where surcharging is permitted, acknowledgement of any surcharge assessed and the associated disclosures.
- Where surcharging is permitted, acknowledgement of any surcharge assessed and the associated disclosures.
- Provide an online cancellation procedure if the Cardholder's request for goods or services was initially accepted online.
- Not include partial payment for goods or services purchased in a single Transaction.
- Not include additional finance charges on a Recurring Transaction.
- Obtain an Authorization for each Transaction in the series.
- Not complete a Recurring Transaction beyond the duration expressly authorized by the Cardholder or if it receives either a Decline Response or a cancellation notice from the Cardholder.
- Not resubmit a Preauthorized Transaction for Authorization more than 4 times within 16 calendar days from the date of the original Decline Response, only if the Decline Response is one of the following Response Codes:
    - 05 (Authorization declined);
    - 51 (Insufficient funds);
    - 61 (Exceeds approval amount limit);
    - 65 (Exceeds withdrawal frequency limit).
- Not resubmit a Transaction for Authorization if the Transaction receives a Pickup Response, or a Decline Response of Response Code 54 (Expired Card),

Response Code 14 (Invalid Account Number [no such number]), or Response Code 57 (Transaction not permitted).

5.10 Transaction Receipt Requirements

5.10.1 Transaction Receipt Delivery to Cardholders

5.10.1.2 Electronic Format Cardholder Receipt Delivery Requirements

If a Merchant offers an Electronic Format Cardholder Receipt instead of a paper Transaction Receipt, the Merchant must do all of the following:

- Inform the Cardholder of the delivery method (for example: email, wirelessly delivered message, link in a wirelessly delivered message) of the receipt and when it will be sent.
- Provide the receipt in a static format that cannot be easily manipulated after it has been created.
- If a link to a website is provided, provide clear instructions to the Cardholder for accessing the receipt on the website.
- Provide instructions to enable the Cardholder to obtain the receipt if the Cardholder does not receive it.
- Make the receipt available to the Cardholder for at least 24 hours after the Transaction is completed.
- Not store or use personal information provided by the Cardholder to enable the Merchant to provide the receipt for any other purpose without the express consent of the Cardholder.
- Include both of the following in the title of the email or the title or first line of the wirelessly-delivered message:
    - The Merchant name as it will appear in the Clearing Record and on the Cardholder billing statement;
    - Language indicating that the email or wirelessly-delivered message contains the Cardholder's copy of a Transaction Receipt or a link to the Cardholder's copy of a Transaction Receipt.

5.10.3.2 Required Transaction Receipt Content for All Transactions

A Transaction Receipt must include all of the following elements:

Required Element	Additional Requirements
Account Number or Token	The Account Number or Token, except for the final 4 digits, must be disguised or suppressed on the Cardholder's copy of a Transaction Receipt.
Authorization Code	Applies only to Transactions that were authorized by the Issuer
Card network name	Must contain "Visa"
Description of goods or services	Description of the purchase. This does not apply to Cash Disbursements.
Merchant location	Merchant city and state/province
Merchant name	The name the Merchant uses to identify itself to its customers - For a Transaction involving a Payment Facilitator or High-Risk Internet Payment Facilitator, the Payment Facilitator and Sponsored Merchant name (or an abbreviation)
Return and refund policies	As specified in Section 5.4.2.4, "Disclosure to Cardholders of Return and Refund Policies"

Transaction amount and Transaction currency symbol	Total currency amount of all goods and services sold to the Cardholder at the same time, including applicable taxes and fees and any adjustments or credits. The currency symbol denoting the Transaction Currency must be included. If currency symbol or currency identifier is not included, the transaction currency is set to the currency of the transaction country by default.
Transaction Date	Transaction Date
Transaction type	One of the following: - ATM Cash Disbursement - Cash-Back with no purchase - Credit - Manual Cash Disbursement - Prepaid Load - Purchase

5.10.3.3 Required Transaction Receipt Content for Specific Transaction Types

In addition to the requirements in Section 5.10.3.2, "Required Transaction Receipt Content for All Transactions," a Transaction Receipt must contain all of the following, as applicable:

Transaction type	Required Content
Aggregated Transaction	- Amount of each individual purchase - Date of each individual purchase

	• Description of each individual purchase
Cruise Line Transaction	• Cabin rate • Dates of embarkation and disembarkation • For No Show Transactions, the words "No Show"
Delayed Delivery Transaction	The words "Deposit" and "Balance," as appropriate
Electronic Commerce Transactions	• Customer service contact • Merchant country • Conditions of sale, including return and cancellation policy
Government Payments (CEMEA Region)	Amount of Government Payment (clearly and separately disclosed from the Service Fee)
Hotel	• Dates of check-in and check-out • Room rate • For No Show Transactions, the words "No Show"
Quasi-Cash Transaction	• 4 digits printed below the Card number • Secondary Cardholder identification information
Recurring Transaction	• The words "Recurring Transactions" • Frequency of Recurring Transactions

	• Duration of Recurring Transaction period

3.3.5. Payment Facilitator

5.3 Payment Facilitators

5.3.1 Acquirer Responsibilities and Liabilities in Payment Facilitator Agreements

5.3.1.1 Required Content of Payment Facilitator Agreement

The Acquirer must include all of the following in a Payment Facilitator Agreement:

- A requirement that the Payment Facilitator enter into a contract with each Sponsored Merchant;
- The Acquirer's right to immediately terminate a Sponsored Merchant or the Payment Facilitator for good cause or fraudulent or other activity or upon Visa request;
- Statements specifying that the Payment Facilitator:
    - Is liable for all acts, omissions, Cardholder disputes, and other Cardholder customer service-related issues caused by the Payment Facilitator's Sponsored Merchants;
    - Is responsible and financially liable for each Transaction processed on behalf of the Sponsored Merchant, or for any disputed Transaction or credit;
    - Must not transfer or attempt to transfer its financial liability by asking or requiring Cardholders to waive their dispute rights;
    - Must not transfer or attempt to transfer its financial liability by asking or requiring Cardholders to waive their dispute rights;
    - Must not deposit Transactions on behalf of another Payment Facilitator;
    - Must not contract with a Sponsored Merchant whose contract was terminated at the direction of Visa or a government agency;
    - Must not deposit Transactions from Sponsored Merchants outside the Acquirer's jurisdiction;

- Must provide the names of principals and their country of domicile for each of its Sponsored Merchants and Transaction reports to its Acquirer and to Visa upon request;
- Must ensure that its Sponsored Merchants comply with the Payment Card Industry Data Security Standard (PCI DSS) and the Payment Application Data Security Standard (PA-DSS).

5.3.1.2 Acquirer Monitoring of Payment Facilitator and Sponsored Merchant Activity

A Sponsored Merchant will be treated as a Merchant of its Payment Facilitator's Acquirer.

An Acquirer that contracts with a Payment Facilitator is liable for all acts, omissions, and other adverse conditions caused by the Payment Facilitator and its Sponsored Merchants, including, but not limited to:

- Related legal costs;
- Settlement to the Payment Facilitator or Sponsored Merchant.

The acts and omissions caused by a Sponsored Merchant will be treated as those of the Payment Facilitator and those caused by a Payment Facilitator or a Sponsored Merchant as those of the Acquirer.

An entity that deposits a Transaction, receives settlement from, or contracts with an Acquirer on behalf of a Merchant is classified as a Merchant if all of the following apply:

- The entity represents itself as selling the goods or services to the Cardholder.
- The entity uses its name primarily to identify its Merchant Outlet to the Cardholder.
- The entity provides recourse to the Cardholder in the event of a dispute.

Otherwise, the entity is classified as a Payment Facilitator.

Visa reserves the right to determine whether an entity is a Payment Facilitator or a Merchant and may use additional criteria including, but not limited to, the entity's name that appears on the Transaction Receipt and the entity that:

- Owns or takes possession of the goods or services;
- Books the sale as revenue;
- Provides customer service and handles returns.

An entity that acts as both a Payment Facilitator and a Merchant must comply with Payment Facilitator rules when acting as a Payment Facilitator and with Merchant rules when acting as a Merchant.

5.3.1.3 Acquirer Responsibilities Regarding Payment Facilitators

If an Acquirer contracts with a Payment Facilitator, it must comply with all of the following:

- Be in good standing in all Visa risk management programs;
- Be financially sound (as determined by Visa);
- Meet a minimum equity requirement.
- Ensure that its registration of its Payment Facilitator, including the name the Payment Facilitator uses to identify itself in the Merchant name field and the attestation of due diligence review, is confirmed by Visa before submitting Transactions on behalf of the Payment Facilitator or its Sponsored Merchant. If the Payment Facilitator is considered to be high-brand risk, it must be registered as a High-Risk Internet Payment Facilitator even if that Payment Facilitator has previously been registered with Visa.
- If the Payment Facilitator's annual Transaction volume in the Acquirer's jurisdiction exceeds USD 50 million, additional requirements apply (detailed in source document).
- Not allow its Payment Facilitator to provide payment services to the following merchant types:
    - Internet pharmacies;
    - Outbound telemarketers.
- Upon Visa request, submit to Visa activity reporting on its Payment Facilitator's Sponsored Merchants that includes all of the following for each Sponsored Merchant:
    - Sponsored Merchant name as it appears in the Merchant name field

- Sponsored Merchant DBA name
- Payment Facilitator name
- Monthly Transaction count and amount
- Monthly Chargeback count and amount

- Ensure that its Sponsored Merchants and the Sponsored Merchants of its Payment Facilitators follow all Merchant-related rules.
- Ensure that its Payment Facilitators provide customer service directly or through its Sponsored Merchants.

5.3.2 Payment Facilitator Responsibilities and Requirements.

5.3.2.2 Payment Facilitator Location

The location of a Payment Facilitator is either the:

- Payment Facilitator's principal place of business.
- Country in which all of the following occur, if the Payment Facilitator operates in multiple countries:
  - The Payment Facilitator uses a local address for correspondence and judicial process.
  - The Payment Facilitator pays taxes related to revenue earned from the provision of the Payment Facilitator's Card acceptance services to Sponsored Merchants, if the country levies such taxes.
  - The Payment Facilitator maintains a bank account into which is paid revenue earned from the provision of the Payment Facilitator's services to Sponsored Merchants.
  - The Payment Facilitator is subject to local laws and regulations.

Self-control questions

1. Give a definition for Payment Facilitator.
2. Explain the concept of the term Sponsored Merchant.
3. What do the abbreviations PAN and BIN stand for?
4. What are MID, TID, MCC and Descriptor?
5. What is the basic postulate of the legitimacy of transaction?
6. In cases where Visa rules conflict with local laws, what takes precedence?
7. Where should the Payment Facilitator be in relation to its Acquirer? Where can Sponsored Merchant be in relation to Acquirer?
8. Who is responsible for the actions and inaction of Merchant's and Sponsored Merchant's?
9. What is the time frame for Visa cards for sending Authorization Reversal?
10. List the requirements for a Merchant website.
11. Can a Merchant display the card number in full?
12. List the elements that should be contained in the e-commerce Merchant's receipt.

4. Technical integration

In the context of technical interaction, all the processing (PSP) on the Internet works in two ways:

- by accepting payment on its payment page,
- by giving a merchant direct access to a payment gateway, allowing implementation of the payment page on its side (API).

Depending on the number of transactions per year, the second of the described methods places a requirement on processing of either filling in a PCI DSS questionnaire and conducting quarterly scans for compliance with security requirements, or obtaining a PCI DSS certificate (this aspect will be discussed below). The acquiring banks prefer to work with merchants by using the first method, as it allows acquirers or their agents to control the domains that the payment page appears at (merchants are not allowed to substitute sites), and also to ensure the safety of payers' card data.

At the time of transfer to a payment form or directly through a gateway, processing provides each merchant with the following set of operations: charge-offs, refunds and recurring payments. Most of the operations performed during processing, which we will call derivatives for convenience, are variations of base operations.

Without going into the technical details of interaction protocols, we will consider various payment operations below.

4.1. Basic Operations

Basic operations are those that payment systems provide to their participants.

Authorization is the process in which a merchant receives permission from the issuing bank to effect payment. The authorization includes an assessment of the risk of conducting a transaction with the card, and, if approved, it reserves the amount of the purchase price on the Cardholder's account.

This is how it works:

- The Cardholder makes a purchase and pays with a card.
- The Merchant sends a transaction requesting authorization to its Acquiring Bank.
- The Acquirer sends an authorization request to the Payment System.
- The Payment System sends a request to the Issuing Bank.
- The Issuing Bank either approves or rejects the transaction.
- The Payment System forwards the response of the Issuing Bank to the Acquirer.
- The Acquiring Bank sends the response to the Merchant.

As we already know, in order to complete the authorization, i. e. to charge-off the money from the buyer's account, the transaction should be sent to clearing. Authorization and clearing are often called two phases of authorization. In Visa system, Base I is responsible for the first phase, and Base II is responsible for the second.

Actually, the authorization holds (or reserves) funds on the client's card. The time during which money can be held depends on both the type of transaction and the type of card. For example, in electronic commerce for transactions conducted with Visa Electron cards, money can be held for no more than 6 days. After the holding time expires, the issuing bank "unfreezes" (or returns) the money to the cardholder's account.

In case a transaction is sent for clearing after the expiration of the time established by IPS for the card, the issuing bank has the right to chargeback, which is called "Late Presentment".

Reversal is a request to the issuing bank from the cardholder to release the reserved amount, sent before the actual write-off of funds from the cardholder's account. This can happen in the event that the cardholder has changed his mind about making an order, or the merchant can not fulfill this order. The reversal can be full or partial. Additionally, the reversal can be initiated by the merchant itself or by the processing system. Reversal is possible only until the moment a transaction is sent to clearing.

For transactions initiated with Visa cards in Card-Absent Environment this period is as follows:
- 72 hours of the original authorization.

- 7 calendar days of the original authorization request if the final transaction amount is less than the authorized amount.

For MasterCard, according to the rules established for the European region, a request for a full or partial reversal must be sent within 24 hours.

If a reversal is performed at the end of the time period established by the IPS, it is likely that it will be rejected.

Refund. A refund transfers funds from merchant account back to the cardholder's bank account. Refunds are always associated with a transaction that has been authorized and settled. Refunds can be initiated at cardholder's or merchant's request, or they can be system generated. In this case, a refund is possible within one year from transaction processing.

Account Funding Transaction (AFT) method pulls funds from a sender's account, in preparation for pushing funds to a recipient's account.

Original Credit Transaction (OCT) credits (pushes) funds to a recipient's Visa account.

4.2. Derived operations

Derived operations are those that implement final processing directly for merchants. They are variations of the above-mentioned basic operations. Thus, Recurrent is essentially the basic authorization request with an addition of "R" flag.

Let's take a look at such operations using a conventional gateway as an example:

Purchase is the operation of debiting funds from the buyer's card that consists of basic authorization and subsequent sending of transaction to clearing. Although technically a clearing file (an array of data containing information about daily transactions) is sent out only in the evening, many acquiring banks allow only Refund operations and charge a commission for authorization.

Authorization, which is sometimes also called pre-authorization (Pre-Auth), is equivalent to basic authorization.

Confirm (confirmation of authorization) is the operation of sending a transaction for clearing.

Recurring payments.

Recurring transactions refer to the instance when consumers authorize merchants to charge their credit card or debit cards a specific amount on a regular basis – such as monthly, quarterly or yearly – for a series of goods or regular services.

In order to initiate recurring payments an initial transaction is needed. An initial transaction is needed to store the card data at processing system. All subsequent charge-offs will be conducted as a sort of basic authorization, but without the need to enter CVV.

Many banks require that an initial transaction be conducted with 3-D Secure in order to reduce the risks of fraud (this technology will be discussed in detail later on in "Risks" chapter).

The responsibility for periodic withdrawal of funds without the cardholder's participation is directly laid on processing, which has to send authorization to the acquiring bank at specified periods of time and for a fixed amount of money.

Recurrent billing (or Rebilling) is when a merchant automatically charges a cardholder for specified goods or services on a prearranged schedule. In other words, the schedule and the amount of charge-off is in this case are determined by the merchant.

4.3. PCI DSS

The Payment Card Industry Data Security Standard (PCI DSS), which was mentioned at the beginning of the book, is a data security standard for payment card industry, developed by the Payment Card Industry Security Standards Council (PCI SSC), established by international payment systems Visa, MasterCard, American Express, JCB and Discover. The standard is a set of 12 detailed requirements to ensure the security of data on the holders of payment cards, which is transmitted, stored and processed in the information infrastructures of these organizations. The adoption of appropriate measures for compliance with the requirements of the standard implies an integrated approach to ensuring information security of payment cards data.

About the Payment Card Industry Data Security Standard

The requirements of the standard apply to all companies that work with international payment systems Visa and MasterCard. Depending on the number of transactions processed, each company is assigned a certain level with a corresponding set of requirements that mandatory to perform. The standard mandates annual audits of companies and quarterly network scanning.

The standard brings together the requirements for information protection of a number of international payment systems:

MasterCard – Site Data Protection (SDP); Visa USA – Cardholder Information Security (CISP); Visa Europe – Account Information Security (AIS).

Starting from September 2006, the standard has been introduced by the Visa international payment system as compulsory for CEMEA region, which includes Russia. All service providers (processing centers, payment gateways, Internet providers) working directly with VisaNet must pass the audit procedure for compliance with the requirements of the standard.

PCI DSS certification

Various international payment systems have their own requirements for the PCI DSS certification process. There are different levels of certification for merchants and for service providers.

The following methods for verifying compliance with the PCI DSS standard are in operation worldwide:

- external QSA-audit (Qualified Security Assessor) performed by a PCI QSA company at the premises of the audited organization;
- submitting the Self-Assessment Questionnaire (SAQ);
- automated ASV scan of network vulnerabilities.

The exact method of checking for compliance, or a combination of thereof, depends on the level of certification of merchant or service provider.

Levels of certification for merchants

Visa classification:

Level 1:

- merchants processing over 6 million transactions per year.

Certification requirements:

- annual audit performed by QSA auditor at organization premises;
- quarterly ASV scanning.

Level 2:

- merchants processing from 1 to 6 million transactions per year.

Certification requirements:

- annual compliance self-assessment with SAQ;
- quarterly ASV scanning.

Level 3:

- merchants processing between 20,000 and 1 million transactions per year using e-commerce tools.
- merchants classified by Visa international payment system as Level 3.

Certification requirements:

- annual compliance self-assessment with SAQ;
- quarterly ASV scanning.

Level 4:

- All other merchants.

Certification requirements:

- annual compliance self-assessment with SAQ is recommended;
- quarterly ASV scanning is recommended;
- the requirements are determined by the acquiring bank.

Levels of certification for service providers

Service providers are organizations that provide various services (mainly in the field of information technology) to merchants, acquiring banks and issuers, as well as directly to international payment systems. Service providers get access to cardholder's data. Examples of service providers include: processing centers, payment gateways, data centers, tokenization and point-to-point encryption (P2PE) service providers.

Visa classification:

Level 1:

- All processing centers connected to VisaNet;
- Service providers processing, storing or transmitting data on more than 300,000 transactions per year.

Certification requirements:

- annual audit performed by QSA auditor at organization premises;
- quarterly ASV scanning.

Level 2:

- Service providers that process, store, or transmit data on less than 300,000 transactions per year.

Certification requirements:

- annual compliance self-assessment with SAQ;
- quarterly ASV scanning.

MasterCard classification:

Level 1:

- All processing centers.
- Service providers processing, storing or transmitting data on more than 300,000 transactions per year.
- All processing centers and service providers operating systems that had compromised cardholders data.

Certification requirements:

- annual audit performed by QSA auditor at organization premises;
- quarterly ASV scanning.

Level 2:

- Service providers processing, storing or transmitting data on less than 300,000 transactions per year.

Certification requirements:

- annual compliance self-assessment with SAQ;
- quarterly ASV scanning.

PCI QSA auditing companies

As can be seen from the classification, certification at the highest levels should be conducted by an auditing company with the status of Qualified Security Assessor (PCI QSA). For the remaining levels, QSA involvement of is not a mandatory requirement. However, QSA can provide consulting services for certification at any level.

PCI DSS Requirements

PCI DSS defines the following six control areas and 12 basic safety requirements.

1. Build and Maintain a Secure Network
- Requirement 1: Install and maintain a firewall configuration to protect cardholder data. - Requirement 2: Do not use vendor-supplied defaults for system passwords and other security parameters.
1. Protect Cardholder Data
- Requirement 3: Protect stored cardholder data. - Requirement 4: Encrypt transmission of cardholder data across open, public networks.
1. Maintain a Vulnerability Management Program
- Requirement 5: Use and regularly update anti-virus software or programs. - Requirement 6: Develop and maintain secure systems and applications.

1. Implement Strong Access Control Measures

- Requirement 7: Restrict access to cardholder data by business need-to-know.
- Requirement 8: Assign a unique ID to each person with computer access.
- Requirement 9: Restrict physical access to cardholder data.

1. Regularly Monitor and Test Networks

- Requirement 10: Track and monitor all access to network resources and cardholder data.
- Requirement 11: Regularly test security systems and processes.

1. Maintain an Information Security Policy

- Requirement 12: Maintain a policy that addresses information security for employees and contractors.

Self-control questions

1. What are two main ways to integrate merchants into a payment gateway?
2. What is authorization?
3. What operation cancels authorization? During what period of time is it possible?
4. What does Refund do?
5. What is AFT?
6. What is OCT?
7. How does Pre-Authorization work?
8. What is a recurring transaction?
9. Why was the PCI DSS standard developed?
10. What does PCI DSS stand for?
11. How often should a merchant pass a PCI DSS audit?
12. How often should a processing center pass a PCI DSS audit?

5. Risks

5.1. Acquirer's Responsibility

Each Visa participant Member is solely responsible for its issuance of Visa products and acquiring of Merchants to accept Visa products, including responsibility for settlement of Transactions, compliance with the Visa Charter Documents and the Visa International Operating Regulations, and ensuring that their Visa programs comply with all applicable legal and regulatory requirements. (Visa Core Rules, Section 1.1.9.1 "Taking Responsibility")

Let us recall that "An Acquirer that contracts with a Payment Facilitator is liable for all acts, omissions, and other adverse conditions caused by the Payment Facilitator and its Sponsored Merchants, including, but not limited to:

- Related legal costs;
- Settlement to the Payment Facilitator or Sponsored Merchant."

It should be understood that, in fact, the Acquirer bears primary responsibility before the Association for any actions of Merchants, Payment Facilitators and Sponsored Merchants. The Association imposes fines on the Acquirer, and then the Acquirer, on the basis of his agreements with Merchants, Payment Facilitators and Sponsored Merchants, can delegate those fines on to them.

5.2. Dispute Resolution.

5.2.1. Chargeback

Chargeback is the procedure of protesting a transaction initiated by the issuing bank for consumer protection, that results in payment amount being directly debited from the recipient (acquirer bank) and returned to the payer, after which the burden of proof lies with the merchant.

Chargebacks are governed by a series of rules described in section 11 of Visa Rules.

Transaction stages:
- For Visa:

    1. First presentment (Initial Transaction)
    2. First Chargeback
    3. Second presentment (Representment)
    4. Pre-Arbitration
    5. Arbitration

- For MasterCard

    1. First presentment (Initial Transaction)
    2. First Chargeback
    3. Second presentment (Representment)
    4. Second Chargeback
    5. Arbitration

First presentment

Initial transaction is a purchase of goods or services.

First Chargeback

Chargeback can be initiated by the issuing bank or by card holder. Occasionally this is done trough Retrieval request by the card-issuing bank requesting a copy of the transaction receipt[13]. Retrieval request helps determine the validity of cardholder's claims for chargeback.

Upon receiving retrieval request the following takes place:

- Upon notification of the retrieval request, a letter is automatically generated to the merchant. This letter states that the merchant has a certain number of days (usually 10 days) to respond by providing the indicated sales draft.
- On the 11th day, a second and last letter is generated, and sent to the merchant. The sales draft must be submitted to the Issuer within 30 days from the moment the request has been initiated.

In other words, a cardholder writes a letter or fills in the Dispute Resolution Form and sends this information to his card-issuing bank. The Issuing Bank then processes a chargeback along with the "Chargeback Documentation" (i. e. Cardholder letter) through the corresponding Association (Visa or MasterCard) and thus is credited the disputed transaction amount.

The Acquirer or "Merchant Bank" then receives notification of the Chargeback and is subsequently debited for the disputed transaction amount. At this point the Acquirer internal database assesses the Merchant a "Chargeback fee" Acquirer's systems then run the chargeback through a series of simple filters to check to see if the Merchant issued credit and for certain technical errors. At this point one of two scenarios occurs:

- If, via the filters, the Chargeback is deemed invalid, Acquirer "Reverses" the Chargeback back through the Association and eventually back to the Issuing Bank along with a debit for the disputed amount. The Acquirer is then credited for the amount in dispute. The Chargeback fee remains on the Merchant's account as this is a fee charged by the Associations as a cost for processing the Chargeback. This "First Chargeback" phase of the dispute is then considered "Resolved To the Issuing Bank" and will remain closed unless the Issuing Bank initiates a "Pre-Arbitration" notification (Visa) or a Second Chargeback (MasterCard).
- If, via the filters, the Chargeback is deemed valid, the Merchant's business checking account is immediately debited for the amount in dispute and a letter is sent to the Merchant the same day advising of the debit and explaining what, if any, documentation is required to "Reverse" this Chargeback. This "First Chargeback" phase of the dispute is then considered "Resolved to the Merchant" and will remain closed until the Merchant responds back to the letter sent to them.

Second Presentment / Representment (First Reversal)

If the merchant does indeed respond with a "Merchant Letter" back to the Acquirer, a "Reversal Phase" of the dispute is opened and a Chargebacks Analyst will review the Merchant Letter and will see if the merchant's response and the overall dispute qualify to be "Reversed" back to the Issuing Bank.

At this point, one of two scenarios will occur:

If the Chargebacks Analyst deems the Merchant's response as invalid, they will close out this phase as "Request Denied" and will mail a letter to the Merchant explaining why the Chargeback cannot be reversed back to the Issuing Bank at that time.

If the Chargeback Analyst deems the Merchant's response as valid, the Acquirer "Reverses" the Chargeback back through the Association and eventually back to the Issuing Bank along with a debit for the disputed amount. The Acquirer is then credited for the amount in dispute and in turn credits the Merchant's business checking account. The Chargeback fee remains on the Merchant's account as this is a fee charged by the Associations as a cost for processing the Chargeback. This "First Reversal" phase of the dispute is then considered "Resolved To the Issuing Bank" and will remain closed unless the Issuing Bank initiates a "Pre- Arbitration" notification (Visa) or a Second Chargeback (MasterCard).

Each stage lasts for 45 days since the chargeback's date of processing. The time period is calculated from the day following the day of chargeback processing, a Second Presentation and Pre-Arbitration. Sending the necessary documentation at all stages is to be done within 5 days from the date of chargeback processing for Visa and 8 days for MasterCard.

Second Chargeback and Second Reversal Phase (only for MasterCard)

Once a Reversal (and the subsequent debit) is received back at the Issuing Bank, they will then forward the "Merchant's Letter" back to their Cardholder for a response. If the Cardholder wishes to pursue the dispute further, they then send in a "Rebuttal Letter" back to the Issuing Bank and if the Issuing Bank feels that their response is valid, will submit a Second Chargeback. A Second Chargeback functions just like a First Chargeback, except a Chargeback fee is not assessed and the disputed amounted is immediately debited out of the Merchant's business checking account. The Merchant is sent another letter explaining what, if any, documentation is required to pursue this dispute further. This "Second Chargeback" phase of the dispute is then considered "Resolved to the Merchant" and will remain closed until the Merchant responds back to the letter sent to them. If the Merchant does indeed respond to the letter sent to them a '"Second Reversal" phase of the dispute is opened. An Acquirer Chargeback Analyst will then review the letter and one of two scenarios will occur:

- If the Chargeback Analyst deems the Merchant's response as invalid, they will close out this phase as "Request Denied" and will mail a letter to the Merchant explaining why the Chargeback cannot be pursued further at that time.
- If the Chargeback Analyst deems the Merchant's response as valid, they will submit a "Pre-Arbitration" letter directly to the Issuing back advising that the Acquirer believes the Merchant's claim is valid and that Acquirer will request MasterCard to make an Arbitration ruling on the dispute if the Issuer disagrees with the Merchant's claim.

The final stage of the development of events may be as follows:

- If the Issuing Bank agrees with the Merchant's claim, they will simply forward the funds back to the Acquirer and the Acquirer will then credit the Merchant's business checking account accordingly. The dispute at this point is considered "Successful" and cannot be re-opened.
- If the Issuing Bank disagrees with the Merchant's claim, they will send a letter back to the Acquirer advising of such. The Acquirer will then send a form to the Merchant requesting that they sign the form which makes the Merchant liable for Arbitration filing fees. When MasterCard makes an Arbitration ruling, it assesses a $400 filing fee to the loser of the dispute. If the Merchant does not agree to the fees, the Acquirer simply closes out the Second Reversal phase of the case as "Unsuccessful". If the Merchant does indeed agree to the fees and submits the signed form, the Acquirer then submits an Arbitration Request to MasterCard directly. If MasterCard rules in the Merchant's favor, the Issuer is immediately debited and the Acquirer is credited for the amount in dispute and forwards the credit to the Merchant's business checking account. The Issuing Bank is also assessed the filing fees and the Acquirer closes this phase of the dispute as "Successful" If MasterCard rules in the Issuer's favor, the amount in dispute remains on its account and the Acquirer is assessed the $400 in filing fees, and will then debit the Merchant's business checking account accordingly.

Issuing Bank Pre-Arbitration Phase (Visa only)

Once a Reversal (Second Presentment) is received back at the Issuing Bank, they will then forward the "Merchant's Letter" back to their Cardholder for a response. If the Cardholder wishes to pursue the dispute further, they then send in a "Rebuttal Letter" back to the Issuing Bank and if the Issuing Bank feels that their response is valid, will submit a "Pre-Arbitration" letter directly to the Acquirer advising that they feel that their Cardholder's claim is valid that they will request Visa make an Arbitration ruling on the dispute if the Acquirer disagrees with the Cardholder's claim. The Merchant is then sent another letter along with the Cardholder's rebuttal advising that they need to respond within 10 days. If the Merchant does not respond to the letter within the specified timeframes, the Acquirer Chargeback Analyst will credit the Issuing Bank back for the disputed amount and in turn debit the Merchant's business checking account. This phase of the dispute will then be closed as "Unsuccessful".

If the merchant does indeed respond within the specified timeframe, one of two scenarios will occur:

- If the Chargeback Analyst deems the Merchant's response as invalid, they will close out this phase as "Request Denied" and will credit the Issuing Bank back for the disputed amount and in turn debit the Merchant's business checking account. The Chargebacks Analyst will also mail a letter to the Merchant explaining why the Chargeback cannot be pursued further at that time.
- If the Chargeback Analyst deems the Merchant's response as valid, the Acquirer will then send a form to the Merchant requesting that they sign the form which makes the Merchant liable for Arbitration filing fees. When Visa makes an Arbitration ruling, it assesses a $400 filing fee to the loser of the dispute. If the Merchant does not agree to the fees, the Acquirer simply closes out the Pre-Arbitration phase of the case as "Unsuccessful" and will credit the Issuing Bank back for the disputed amount and in turn debit the Merchant's business checking account. If the Merchant does indeed agree to the fees and submits the signed form, the Acquirer then responds to the Issuing Bank advising them that they do not agree with the

Cardholder's claim. The Issuing bank then submits an Arbitration Request directly to Visa.
- If Visa rules in the Merchant's favor, all funds remain where they are and in addition, The Issuing Bank is assessed the $400 in filing fees. The Acquirer then closes this phase of the dispute as "Successful"
- If Visa rules in the Issuing Bank's favor, they are immediately credited for the amount in dispute and the Acquirer is immediately debited for the same amount and in turn this amount is immediately debited from the Merchant's business checking account along with the $400 in filing fees. The Acquirer then closes this phase of the dispute as "Unsuccessful".

5.3. Visa chargebacks

In order to successfully defend merchant's interests, a chargeback analyst of the acquiring bank or the payment service provider should know all about the different types of chargebacks and have and understanding of when a chargeback can be recognized as invalid, as well as which supporting documentation is required for a rebuttal.

A comprehensive description of these concepts is found in this document:

https://usa.visa.com/dam/VCOM/download/about-visa/visa-rules-public.pdf,

(Section 11.1.9 «Chargeback Reason Codes»).

We will consider some of these situations in more detail.

30 – Services Not Provided or Merchandise Not Received

Chargeback Conditions:

The Cardholder participated in the Transaction but did not receive the merchandise or services. There might be different reasons for that, however, we will summarize them as follows: the Merchant was unwilling or unable to provide the merchandise or services.

The Chargeback is invalid for any of the following:

- A Transaction in which the Cardholder cancelled the merchandise or service before the expected delivery or service date;
- A Transaction in which merchandise is being held by the Cardholder's country's customs agency;
- A Transaction that the Cardholder states is fraudulent;
- A dispute regarding the quality of merchandise or service rendered;
- A partial prepayment with Delayed Delivery Transaction when the remaining balance was not paid and the Merchant is willing and able to provide the merchandise or services.

Chargeback Time Limit:

If applicable, before initiating a Chargeback, an Issuer must wait 15 calendar days from either:

- The Transaction Date, if the date the services were expected or the delivery date for the merchandise is not specified;
- The date the Cardholder returned or attempted to return the merchandise, if the merchandise was returned due to late delivery.

A Chargeback must be processed no later than 120 calendar days from the Transaction Processing Date. If the merchandise or services were to be provided after the Transaction Processing Date, 120 calendar days from the last date that the Cardholder expected to receive the merchandise or services or the date that the Cardholder was first made aware that the merchandise or services would not be provided. In either case this period is not to exceed 540 calendar days from the Transaction Processing Date.

41 – Cancelled Recurring Transaction (Unsubscribe from regular charges)

Chargeback Conditions:

- The Cardholder withdrew permission to charge the account for a Recurring Transaction or, in the Europe Region, an Installment Transaction.

- The Acquirer or Merchant received notification that, before the Transaction was processed, the Cardholder's account was closed or, in the Europe Region, facilities were withdrawn or the Cardholder deceased.
- An initial membership Transaction was previously charged back and the Cardholder did not expressly renew the membership.

The Chargeback in this situation is invalid only for an Installment Transaction

53 – Not as Described or Defective Merchandise

Chargeback Conditions:

- The Cardholder returned merchandise or cancelled services that did not match what was described on the Transaction Receipt or other documentation presented at the time of purchase;
- The merchandise received by the Cardholder was damaged or defective, and the Cardholder returned the merchandise to the Merchant;
- The Cardholder disputes the quality of the merchandise or services; • The merchandise was identified as counterfeit by: the owner of the intellectual property or its authorized representative; a customs agency, law enforcement agency, or other governmental agency; a neutral bona fide expert.
- The Cardholder claims that the terms of sale were misrepresented by the Merchant.

The Chargeback is invalid for any of the following:

- The Cash-Back portion of a Visa Cash-Back Transaction;
- A dispute regarding Value-Added Tax (VAT);
- A Transaction in which the returned merchandise is held by any customs agency except the Merchant's country's customs agency;
- A dispute related solely to the quality of merchandise or services provided.

Chargeback Time Limit:

Unless otherwise specified, a Chargeback must be processed no later than 120 calendar days from one of the following:

- The Transaction Processing Date;
- For merchandise or services purchased on or before the Transaction Processing Date, the date the Cardholder received the merchandise or services, as well as for merchandise or services provided after the Transaction Processing Date, the date the Cardholder received the merchandise or services;
- For a Delayed Delivery Transaction, the Processing Date of the balance portion of the Transaction;

Before initiating a Chargeback, the Issuer must wait 15 calendar days from the date the merchandise was returned. or the Cardholder attempted to return the merchandise. or the service was cancelled.

A Chargeback must be processed no later than 120 calendar days from the last date that the Cardholder expected to receive the merchandise or services or the date on which the Cardholder was first made aware that the merchandise or services would not be provided, In either case, this period is not to exceed 540 calendar days from the Transaction Processing Date.

There are cases when the processing time is halved. A Chargeback must be processed no later than 60 calendar days from the date the Issuer received the first Cardholder notification of the dispute, if all the following apply:

- There is evidence in the notification of previous ongoing negotiations between the Cardholder and the Merchant to resolve the dispute;
- The above-mentioned negotiations occurred within 120 days of the Transaction Processing Date;
- The Chargeback Processing Date is no later than 540 calendar days from the Transaction Processing Date.

74 – Late Presentment[14]

Chargeback Conditions:

- The Transaction was not processed within the required time limit;
- The Account Number was not in good standing on the Chargeback Processing Date;

- The Transaction Date is more than 180 calendar days before the Processing Date.

The Chargeback applies only if the Transaction Processing Date is more than:

- For a Visa Electron Card Transaction, 6 calendar days after the Transaction Date;
- For an ATM or Load Transaction, 10 calendar days after the Transaction Date;
- For all other Transactions, 30 calendar days after the Transaction Date.

75 – Transaction Not Recognized

Chargeback Conditions:

The Cardholder does not recognize the Transaction and additional information beyond the data required in the Clearing Record is needed to assist the Cardholder in identifying the Transaction

The Chargeback is invalid for any of the following:

- A Transaction for which the Issuer used Retrieval Request reason code 33 (fraud analysis request) or Retrieval Request reason code 34 (legal process request);
- A Transaction for which the Acquirer supplies a Fulfillment with all required data specified in Section 5.10.4.1, "Required Substitute Transaction Receipt Content for T&E/Travel Transactions";
- A Transaction for which the Lodging/Car Rental No-Show indicator in the Clearing Record is 1;
- A Transaction that the Cardholder states is fraudulent;
- A Transaction for which the Acquirer provided evidence of an Imprint;
- A Visa Easy Payment Service Transaction.

80 – Incorrect Transaction Amount or Account Number

Chargeback Conditions:

- The Transaction amount is incorrect or an addition or transposition error occurred;
- The Account Number processed through VisaNet does not match the Account Number on the Transaction Receipt;

The Chargeback is invalid for any of the following:

- A T&E Transaction in which there is a difference between the quoted price and the actual charges made by the Merchant;
- A No-Show or Advance Deposit Transaction.

83 – Fraud – Card-Absent Environment

Chargeback Conditions:

- The Cardholder did not authorize or participate in a Transaction conducted in a Card-Absent Environment;
- A fraudulent Transaction was completed in a Card-Absent Environment using an Account Number for which no valid Card was issued or is outstanding, and no Authorization was obtained.

The Chargeback is invalid for any of the following:

- An Emergency Cash Disbursement;
- A Transaction for which both: The CVV2 result code in the Authorization message is U (Issuer not participating in CVV2 program), and the CVV2 presence indicator in the Authorization Request is one of the following:
    - 1 (CVV2 value is present);
    - 2 (CVV2 value is on the Card but is illegible);
    - 9 (Cardholder states CVV2 is not present on the Card).
- An Electronic Commerce Transaction for which all of the following: The CVV2 presence indicator in the Authorization Request is 1 (CVV2 value is present), The CVV2 results code in the Authorization Request is N (No Match), The Authorization Request was approved,
- A Transaction for which an Authorization was obtained.

86 – Paid by Other Means

Chargeback Conditions:

The Cardholder paid for the same merchandise or service by other means.

The Chargeback is invalid for any of the following:

- The initial payment of a Delayed Delivery Transaction if the balance payment is not authorized and the balance

was not paid by other means;
- Transactions in which payment for services was made to 2 different Merchants, unless there is evidence that the payment was passed from one Merchant to the other (for example: payment from a travel agent to a T&E Merchant).

93 – Merchant Fraud Performance Program

Chargeback Conditions:

- Visa notified the Issuer that the Transaction was identified by the Merchant Fraud Performance Program and the Issuer has not successfully charged back the Transaction under another reason code.

The Chargeback is invalid only for an Emergency Cash Disbursement.

Time Limit for this kind of Chargeback is 120 calendar days from the date of the identification by the Merchant Fraud Performance Program

5.4. Chargebacks Time Limits.

6.4.1. Visa

Visa Reason Code	Reason Code Description	Time Limit
30	Services Not Provided or Merchandise Not Received	120 (*)
41	Cancelled Recurring Transaction	120
53	Not as Described or Defective Merchandise	120 (*)

74	Late Presentment	120
75	Transaction Not Recognized	120
80	Incorrect Transaction Amount or Account Number	120
83	Fraud – Card-Absent Environment	120
86	Paid by Other Means	120
96	Merchant Fraud Performance Program	120 (*)

Unless otherwise specified in Reason Code

5.5. 3-D Secure

3-D Secure is an XML-based protocol designed to serve as an additional security layer for online credit and debit card transactions. It employs two-factor user authentication, however, it does not guarantee the safety and security of money on the payer's card. The technology was developed specifically for Visa payment system and provides security of Internet payments within Verified by Visa (VbV). Services based on this protocol have also been adopted by MasterCard, known as MasterCard SecureCode (MCC), by JCB International (J/Secure) and by AmEx (SafeKey).

3-D Secure adds an additional authentication step for online payments, allowing merchants and banks to verify the identity of cardholder, preventing fraudulent transactions.

3-D Secure does not provide full protection of money in card-not-present (CNP) environment. For example, a one-time password can be intercepted by computer viruses. Not all banks support this technology, so many products and services can be paid for by card without using verification codes.

5.5.1. Early History

Card payment on the Internet. First steps

In mid-1990s, you could make an online payment by simply entering you bank card number and expiration date. By filling out the form fields with this data on a merchant's website a customer thereby confirmed payment for purchase. An authorization request was generated and transferred through the payment system from the acquiring bank to the issuing bank. When entered correctly this data in most cases indicated a positive response from the issuer.

Thus, not only the cardholder could pay for the goods, but also any person to whom these requisite details were available. To protest a transaction, the cardholder had to apply to his issuing bank and demand a refund of the money, alleging that he had not made a purchase. The bank would then initiate a chargeback, the money would return to the cardholder's account, and the merchant's account would be debited accordingly by the acquiring bank. This, of course, has led to numerous cases of friendly fraud abuse (as mentioned earlier), when, after having paid for goods or services, a cardholder would apply for chargeback at his bank. Disputes around such achargebacks often did not end in merchant's favor with the IPS standing up for cardholders.

The IPS, motivated by the desire to stimulate the purchase of goods via the Internet, had initially established such a simple and primitive way of protesting transactions and making refunds. That initially implemented scheme could be compromise in at least four points:

1. The client's computer and browser. At this stage, a hidden keylogger, a virus, or a fake merchant page could intercept the payer's data.
2. The link between the user and his provider. All traffic passing through provider's servers can be intercepted and analyzed.

3. The online store that transmitted the card data to the processing system of the acquiring bank. Card numbers were often stored in merchants' databases and system protocols, merchants' sites could be hacked and controlled by attackers.
4. The host of the acquiring bank, or the processing center providing card processing services. Here, the data was also stored in database and protocols, which potentially exposed them to copying by staff members.

The first carders (fraudsters in the sphere of payment cards) used computer programs called "generators" to produce a sequence of credit card numbers, and then test them to see which were valid accounts. Whenever they succeeded, the merchants suffered significant losses. Therefore, traders began to include leverage potential risks by raising the costs of their goods.

At that time the safety of card data was given too little attention, and the PCI DSS standard was introduced only a decade later. Card numbers were actively used by merchants for customer accounting, printed on checks and sent by e-mail. Naturally, such practices produced a huge field of operation for fraudulent activities.

More security is required: SSL and CVC

The advent of SSL encryption technology and the enhanced HTTPS protocol based on it helped to eliminate card data leakage in communication channels. In addition, for the purpose of entering card data it became possible to transfer customers from merchant's site to a secure site of the processing center of the acquiring bank or PSP.

Additional authentication of cardholder's identity was enforced by payment systems by implementing a special Card Verification Code (CVC). MasterCard member banks started issuing this new type of cards in 1997, and Visa in 2001. CVC was known to the issuer and printed on the back of the card. This innovation was based on the assumption that at the time of transaction, the payer has the card in his hands. Like the PIN code, the CVC was not stored anywhere and was transmitted over communication channels only at the time of authorization.

This measure allowed, on the one hand, to render innocuous card number generators, and on the other, to improve security for online merchants. From now on, once the issuing bank checked the CVC and authorized the transaction, it became difficult to claim it as fraudulent.

Moving to 3-D Secure

Offline payment card fraud was another problem to tackle, which brought issuing banks and payment systems together to start a migration to cards with an embedded microprocessor chips. The development of chip-enabled cards significantly reduced the possibility of their forgery. Having lost the ability to read the magnetic strip, scammers focused on online transactions. Two vectors of attacks became prominent: the customers and the infrastructure of online merchants and processing systems.

These threats were countered with the development of Payment Card Industry Data Security Standard (PCI DSS). As for direct participants – issuers, acquirers and their customers – payment systems started to implement 3-D Secure technology. It provided additional client authentication directly from the issuing bank. Before sending a request for authorization, a client is asked to enter a one-time password into an online form provided by the processing center of the issuing bank. The password is communicated by a bank directly to a cardholder in a number of ways: by SMS message, a value from a table of code variables or from an ATM check, or a predefined password. A merchant would accept payment once the issuer confirmed the client's authentication.

5.5.2. Liability Shift

Merchants are liable for fraudulent transactions. However, the implementation of 3-D Secure protocol resulted in the so-called "liability shift" from merchant to the issuer or even to the cardholder. In other words, if a cardholder attempts to protest a transaction, which has been confirmed by a password (conducted with 3 DS), by claiming that the payment was made without his consent, in most cases the issuer will refuse a chargeback.

This way transactions get a chargeback protection for the

following types of chargebacks:

- Visa: "75 – Cardholder Does Not Recognize Transaction" and "83 – Fraudulent Transactions Card Absent Environment".
- MasterCard: "4837 – Cardholder Not Authorized" and "4863 – Cardholder Not Recognized".

A transaction receives chargeback protection in case the merchant participates in corresponding programs Verified by Visa or MasterCard SecureCode. And even if the issuing bank does not participate in these programs, it is still liable for such transactions.

5.6. Fraud Advice

Fraud advice is a special notice sent by the issuing bank to the acquiring bank informing it that a complaint was received from a cardholder regarding an illegal charge-off in relation to a previously completed payment transaction.

Such notification contains the original payment transaction data that uniquely identifies it and the reason code. Unlike chargeback, fraud advice does not have an extensive list of codes (about ten codes). Visa and MasterCard each have their own code numbering. The main reason for fraud advice in the field of e-commerce is "Card-not-present fraud" code.

In most cases fraud advice leads to chargeback, but not always. Whenever a chargeback claim is impossible due to successful verification with 3-D Secure, or when for some reason a cardholder is not willing to apply for it, the issuing bank sends fraud advice to the acquiring bank. In this case, the chargeback is not forwarded to the merchant. On the one hand, such an arrangement is good for online merchants, since a fraudulent transaction does not produce the chargeback and the fines associated with it. Chargeback statistic is not getting worse, and a merchant does not bear losses for fraudulent transactions. On the other hand, this apparent absence of a problem is what makes fraud advice treacherously tricky. The fact is that the IPS obliges acquirers to keep a record of the number and amounts of fraud advices for each merchant's account just like it is done for chargebacks. This means that whenever an online merchant exceeds certain limits on the number of fraud advices, it becomes a subject to a special surveillance programs of the IPS. Visa calls this program **TC40** (Transaction code 40), and MasterCard calls it **SAFE** (System to Avoid Fraud Effectively). There are several types of monitoring programs, and their limits are region-dependent.

Once a merchant becomes a subject of such surveillance program, it is given several months to solve the issue of fraudulent payments. The exact period is determined by the specific monitoring program applied, but as a rule, if the program parameters are violated for three months in a row and the merchant fails to normalize its fraud advice status, the payment system imposes fines on the acquiring bank, which in turn, leverages penalties against the merchant and has the right to disconnect a noncomplying merchant from the card payments system.

3DS verification technology, which many online merchants mistakenly regard to be a faultless protection against scammers, can not in fact safeguard their business from all the problems associated with fraudulent transactions. 3-D Secure merely allows online stores to avoid losses of the amount associated with the so-called "bad" payment, that's all. This should be always remembered and the additional means of checking and protecting the incoming payments offered by processing, as well as using risk management systems shouldn't neglected.

5.7. Visa Chargeback Monitoring Program

Visa carefully monitors each merchant and takes action when activities may cause undue harm to the goodwill of the Visa system. One issue that regularly threatens Visa's brand is excessive chargeback levels.

The network's Chargeback Monitoring Programs help acquirers identify merchants who have exceeded the Visa chargeback thresholds. Acquirers are expected to help merchants in the Chargeback Monitoring Programs reduce chargebacks, assess fraud controls, review the operating environment, and more. If merchants are involved in one of Visa's Chargeback Monitoring Programs for too long, Visa may require the acquirer to discontinue the merchant agreement. The Global Merchant Chargeback Monitoring Program includes a workout period. This allows merchants an opportunity to get chargebacks under control before becoming fee eligible.

Chargeback Monitoring Programs

The Chargeback Monitoring Programs analyze merchant activity when chargeback thresholds have been breached. To calculate the thresholds, Visa uses a chargeback-to-transaction ratio. In other words, to calculate the chargeback ratio, Visa tallies the current month's chargebacks and divides the number by the current month's Visa transactions. For example, 100 chargebacks issued in June would be divided by 10,000 transactions in June to produce a chargeback-to-transaction ratio of 1%.

Visa's Chargeback Monitoring Program involves three categories:

Global Merchant Chargeback Monitoring Program (GMCMP)

Category	Number of Chargebacks	Number of Transactions	Chargeback Ratio
Global Merchant Chargeback Monitoring Program	At least 200 international chargebacks	At least 200 international transactions	2% ratio of international chargebacks to international transactions within the same month

The Global Merchant Chargeback Monitoring Program includes a workout period. This allows merchants an opportunity to get chargebacks under control before becoming fee eligible. However, Visa reserves the right to withdraw this workout period if the network feels the merchant's activities cause undue harm to Visa's brand. If the merchant changes acquirers while involved with the Global Merchant Chargeback Monitoring Program, the same status will apply with the new acquirer.

Merchant Chargeback Monitoring Program (MCMP)

Visa has different thresholds depending upon where the acquiring bank is geographically located. In particular, merchants from the CEMEA Region may find themselves in the Merchant Chargeback Monitoring Program.

Category	Number of Chargebacks	Number of Transactions	Chargeback Ratio
Global Merchant Chargeback Monitoring Program	At least 100 chargebacks	At least 100 chargebacks	At least 100 basis points (1% chargeback ratio)

The acquirer will receive notification that its merchant has entered the High Brand Risk Merchant Chargeback Monitoring Program. Within 15 calendar days, the acquirer must notify the merchant. If a merchant moves to another region while involved with a different chargeback monitoring program, it will be added to the equivalent category in that region.

High Brand Risk Chargeback Monitoring Program (HBRCMP)

The High Brand Risk Chargeback Monitoring Program was designed to help high-risk merchants keep chargeback thresholds in check. Involvement in this program applies to all high-risk merchants who meet or exceed Visa chargeback thresholds.

Category	Number of Chargebacks	Number of Transactions	Chargeback Ratio
High Brand Risk	At least 100	At least 100	At least 100 basis points

| Chargeback Monitoring Program | chargebacks | transactions | (1% chargeback ratio) |

The acquirer will receive notification that its merchant has entered the High Brand Risk Merchant Chargeback Monitoring Program. Within 15 calendar days, the acquirer must notify the merchant.

Fraud Thresholds

In addition to chargeback thresholds, Visa also has fraud thresholds (by taking into account fraud-advice messages). If merchants breach these predetermined levels, fees and punishments will be enforced.

Visa's Merchant Fraud Programs	
Domestic Merchant Fraud Performance Program	- At least $10,000 in reported fraud - 1% or greater fraud-to-sales ratio
Interregional	- At least 25 reported fraudulent transactions - At least $25,000 in reported fraud - 2.5% or greater fraud-to-sales ratio
Interregional (Excessive)	- At least $250,000 reported fraud - 2.5% or greater fraud-to-sales ratio

The acquirer can terminate a merchant account because of disproportionate fraud activity.

5.8. MasterCard Excessive Chargeback Program

MasterCard carefully scrutinizes each merchant's chargeback activity as part of the Excessive Chargeback Program. Through the use of predetermined chargeback thresholds, acquirers are able to evaluate and predict chargeback risk. The network expects each acquirer to monitor these MasterCard chargeback rates and take action when a merchant has exceeded (or is expected to exceed) the acceptable threshold.

MasterCard can impose fines on the acquirer for exceeding his merchant's established thresholds on chargebacks and/or require the acquirer to disconnect the merchant from the system. In most cases, as in Visa programs, penalties occur if violations are not eliminated for a long period.

Excessive Chargeback Program

To calculate the chargeback-to-transaction ratio, MasterCard tallies the current month's first chargebacks and divides the amount by the number of MasterCard transactions in the previous month. For example, 100 first chargebacks issued in June would be divided by 10,000 transactions in May to produce a chargeback-to-transaction ratio of 1% or 100 basis points.

It is important to note chargeback thresholds are only impacted by first chargebacks. Second chargebacks (also known as pre-arbitration chargebacks) do not affect the chargeback-to-transaction ratio.

Chargeback Monitored Merchant

Category	Number of Chargebacks	Number of Basis Points	Time-line
Chargeback Monitored Merchant	At least 100 chargebacks	At least 100 basis points (1% chargeback	A merchant earns this title at the end of the monthly

		ratio)	review.

If a merchant's chargeback activity exceeds these thresholds, the label Chargeback Monitored Merchant will be applied. The merchant will remain a Chargeback Monitored Merchant until the basis points drop to an acceptable level. There are two categories for thresholds to consider in these calculations: the above illustrates the limits for domestic banks or processing and the below shows the limits for international banks.

Excessive Chargeback Merchant

Category	Number of Chargebacks	Number of Basis Points	Time-line
Excessive Chargeback Merchant	At least 100 chargebacks	At least 150 basis points (1.5% chargeback ratio)	A merchant earns this title if the threshholds are exceeded for two consecutive months (trigger months). The merchant remains in this category until the basis points drop below 150 for two consecutive months.

Within the category of Excessive Chargeback Merchant, there are two additional distinctions.

- A merchant is a Tier 1 Excessive Chargeback Merchant during months one through six.
- If the merchant is still categorized as an Excessive Chargeback Merchant after the sixth month, the next distinction is Tier 2 for months seven through twelve.

If a merchant reaches Tier 2 of the Excessive Chargeback Merchant category, MasterCard may: Advise the acquirer to create an action plan or implement other strategies to reduce the merchant's chargeback-to-transaction ratio. Require the acquirer to undergo a Global Risk Management Program Customer Risk Review.

Fraud Thresholds

In addition to chargeback thresholds, MasterCard also has fraud thresholds. If merchants breach these predetermined levels, fees and punishments will be enforced.

MasterCard's Global Merchant Audit Program (GMAP)	
Tier 1 Violation	• At least $3,000 in reported fraud • Fraud-to-sales ratio between 3% and 4.99%
Tier 2 Violation	• At least $4,000 in reported fraud • Fraud-to-sales ratio between 5% and 7.99%
Tier 3 Violation	• At least $5,000 in reported fraud • Fraud-to-sales ratio greater than 8%

Just like excessive chargeback levels, the acquirer can terminate a merchant account because of disproportionate fraud activity.

5.9. Visa Non-Compliance Assessments

Below you will find brief excerpts from Visa Rules Public that have to do with non-compliance assessments that this organization imposes on its members.

Visa's Right to Impose Non-Compliance Assessments

The Operator of the Payment System has the right to collect fines and apply other penalties in accordance with these Rules. Authorized representatives of Visa are vested with responsibilities for their implementation. These procedures and non-compliance assessments are in addition to enforcement rights available to Visa under other provisions of the Visa Rules, or through other legal or administrative procedures.

General Non-Compliance Assessment Schedule

Violation	Non-Compliance Assessment
First violation of rule	Warning letter with specific date for correction and USD 1,000
Second violation of same rule in a 12-month period after Notification of first violation	USD 5,000
Third violation of same rule in a 12-month period after Notification of first violation	USD 10,000
Fourth violation of same rule in a 12-month period after Notification of first violation	USD 25,000

If the 12-month period is not violation-free and the fines total USD 25,000 or more	Additional non-compliance assessment equal to all non-compliance assessments levied during that 12- month period

Determination of Violation of the Visa Rules

Determination of a violation of the Visa Rules may be made based on either:

- The response from a Member to a Notification of investigation and other available information.
- The Member's failure to respond to a Notification of investigation and to provide all information requested

Notification of Determination of Violation

Visa will notify a Member if it determines that a violation of the Visa Rules has occurred, or if it determines that a violation is continuing to occur, and will specify a date by which the Member must correct the violation. The Notification will advise the Member of all of the following:

- Reasons for such determination
- Non-compliance assessment amount
- Right to appeal the determination and/or the non-compliance assessments for the violation

Non-Compliance Assessment Member Responsibility

A non-compliance assessment is imposed by Visa on a Member. A Member is responsible for paying all non-compliance assessments, regardless of whether it absorbs them, passes them on, or increases them in billing its customer (for example: Cardholder or Merchant). A Member must not represent to its customer that Visa imposes any non-compliance assessment on its customer.

Imposing non-compliance assessment

After sending a relevant notice to a Member, a non-compliance assessment will be imposed by Visa on a Member within the framework of electronic settlements.

Investigation Response Requirement

Visa will notify a Member of an investigation of violation. A Member must respond to and provide information requested by Visa for a Visa Rules violation that is under investigation The Member must submit its response and information, within the time period specified, by mail, courier, facsimile, hand, email, or other electronic delivery method.

Repeated Non-Compliance

Repetitive violations of the Visa Rules incur heavier non-compliance assessments or other actions. A violation of any rule qualifies as a repetitive violation only if the violating Member does not correct it by the date specified in the Notification.

Non-Compliance Assessments for Repetitive Violations

Non-compliance assessments increase for repetitive violations of the Visa Rules within any 12-month period. The 12-month period begins on the date of the most recent Notification of the violation and ends following a 12-month period free of violations of that rule.

Willful Violations of the Visa Rules

In addition to the non-compliance assessments specified in the Visa Rules, a Member found to have willfully violated the Visa Rules, adversely affecting the goodwill associated with the Visa system, brand, products and services, operation of the Visa Systems, or operations of other Members will be subject to a further non-compliance assessment. A violation is considered "willful" if the Member knew, or should have known, or its knowledge can be fairly implied, that its conduct constituted a violation of the Visa Rules.

Enforcement Appeals

A Member may appeal a determination of a violation or non-compliance assessment to Visa, as follows:

- The Member's appeal letter must be received by Visa within 30 days of the Member's receipt of the Notification of the violation or non-compliance assessment.
- The appealing Member must submit with the appeal any new or additional information necessary to substantiate its

request for an appeal.
- A fee of USD 5,000 will be assessed to the Member upon receipt of the appeal. This fee is refundable if the appeal is upheld.

Based on the response from a Member to a Notification of investigation and other available information, Visa will take a decision on the appeal. A Member may submit arguments supporting its position. All decisions are final and not subject to challenge.

List of sources used

- http://financialaffairs.depaul.edu/treasurer/documents/Chargeback%20Procedures%20and%20Fraud%20Prevention.pdf
- https://ru.wikipedia.org/wiki/3-D_Secure
- https://habrahabr.ru/article/270945/
- https://bepaid.by/frod-edvajs-internet-torgovzy/
- https://chargebacks911.com/knowledge-base/visas-chargeback-monitoring-program/
- https://chargebacks911.com/knowledge-base/mastercards-excessive-chargeback-program/

Self-control questions

1. Who is responsible for Payment Facilitator's actions?
2. Who is responsible for paying compensations to Sponsored Merchants?
3. What is chargeback?
4. What are the stages of dispute resolution process in Visa's practice?
5. List the stages of the dispute resolution process in MasterCard's practice?
6. What does Second Presentment mean?
7. What is First Presentment?
8. How does Arbitration take place in the IPS, and what penalties are imposed on the loser of the dispute.
9. What is Chargeback Visa 30 – Services Not Provided or Merchandise Not Received? What are its time limits?
10. Describe the concept and time frame for Chargeback Visa 74 – Late Presentment.
11. What is meant by Chargeback Visa 83 – Fraud – Card-Absent Environment? What are the time limits for it?
12. Who bears the financial responsibility for an online transaction without the use of 3-D Secure?
13. What is 3-D Secure?
14. To what parties does liability shift when using 3-D Secure? What types of chargebacks does it cover?
15. What is Fraud Advice?
16. What is behind the term Global Merchant Chargeback Monitoring Program (GMCMP)?
17. What is Merchant Chargeback Monitoring Program (MCMP)?
18. Provide the definition of Fraud Thresholds.
19. Explain the meaning of the term Chargeback Monitored Merchant.

6. The cost of Conducting Internet payments

6.1. Overview

In 1958, BofA launched the BankAmericard credit card system, the predecessor of Visa. The bank simultaneously assumed two different functions: emission of cards (for holders) and acquiring (for merchants). In this position the bank set the size of the commission, which it charged both from cardholders and from merchants the post-transactional rate (also known as merchant discount rate).

In 1966, BofA also launched a franchising system. The banks that joined BofA were free to set their own rates for servicing merchants and cardholders. This way, when a buyer holding a card from Bank A made a purchase from a merchant serviced by the same bank, Bank A could apply an interest system similar to that of Bank of America. But in the event that a buyer holding a card from Bank A made a purchase from a merchant serviced by Bank B, Bank of America required that the entire merchant discount would be transferred to Bank A. In practice, this rule meant that the acquiring bank would not receive any profit on transactions with cards from other issuing banks.

In 1970, the BankAmericard system was transformed into an independent organization, National BankAmericard Inc. (NBI), managed by member banks. A year later, NBI introduced Interchange fee for transactions in which different banks acted as issuers and acquirers. This fee was paid by the acquiring bank to the issuing bank and initially was set to 1.95%. At the same time, the acquiring bank had the right to set its merchant discount, which exceeded the interchange fee in order to cover its expenses and make profit. Thus within Visa system there were two possible sources of profit: cardholders and merchants.

MasterCard's arrangements were of a similar nature.

6.2. Transaction Cost

The transaction cost for merchants (discount rate) is set as a percentage of the payment amount, and sometimes a fixed sum is added to that percentage. The commission is charged for a successful authorization, and sometimes it is also charged for rejected authorization. Refunds and chargebacks may also be subject to additional commissions.

In Russia, in most cases, a percentage of the transaction sum is debited for successful authorization.

In Europe a certain fixed rate is often added to the interest rate, and it can be broken down into individual transactions (authorization, clearing, etc.). High-risk merchants are often charged for rejected transactions as well as for refunds and chargebacks.

Example:

Discount rate: 2.5% + 0.08 EURO

Chargeback fee: 20 EURO

Refund fee: 10 EURO

The cost is comprised of two main components: the acquiring bank's commission and the commission of Third Party Agents (TPA) involved in the transaction chain.

For example, in a standard scheme of working with banks, the total commission is a sum of the Acquirer's and the TPA's commissions. When crediting a merchant (settlement), an acquirer immediately debits its commission from the total amount. As for the TPA's commission, it can be either included in the acquirer's rate, or charged separately. In the first case, the acquirer performs settlement with TPA, and in the second case, the client is invoiced at the end of month.

As for the TPA commissions, the arrangement is quite straightforward: they are calculated as a percentage from the turnover or some fixed amount. The so-called "ladder" principle is often used, when the percentage of commission decreases with the growth of turnover and increases with its demise.

The acquirer's commission is calculated according to more complex formulas and is comprised of several components: the interchange fee, the IPS commission and the interest rate of the acquiring bank itself.

6.3. Interchange Fee

Interchange Reimbursement Fee (IRF) is a commission that the financial institutions involved in servicing bank cards pay to each other in the process of performing transactions. Normally it's a fee paid by the merchant's acquirer to the client's issuing bank. However, in some cases the opposite takes place when a payment for an exchange is received by the acquirer from the issuer.

When conducting a bank card transaction, the issuing bank subtracts the IRF from the amount it pays to the merchant's acquiring bank.

These fees are set by Visa and MasterCard payment systems. The IRF price formation is complex and varies with the type of card being used (Classic, Premium, etc.), region and jurisdiction, whether the card is credit or debit, as well as the type and scale of the merchant's enterprise, and the route of transaction (online, MO/TO, etc.). For example, the IRF rates for Premium cards, which assume certain privileges for their holder, will usually be higher than for Classic cards. Transactions with credit cards often have higher rates than with Premium cards. Sales made in card-not-present environment, such as orders by phone or on the Internet, are also subject to higher IRF than transactions conducted in the presence of the cardholder (on POS terminals). It is also important to note that IRF rates, in fact, serve as a mechanism for encouraging the emission of certain type of cards.

Were it not for the IRF, the issuing bank would have to cover the card maintenance expenses (such as fraud prevention, equipment maintenance, cardholder support, etc.). In that case, the bank would have to increase the card servicing cost the for cardholder or stop issuing them altogether.

These rates are constantly monitored and regulated, they are raised or lowered in order to maintain a competitive offer for all parties. The IRF rates should be encouraging the emission and the use of cards, as well as increasing the variety of business accepting payment cards. If the rates are too high, the merchants will not want to accept cards. If the rates are too low, the issuing banks will not want to issue cards.

As mentioned above, IRF vary depending on the type of card, region and jurisdiction. In some regions, the information on IRF is open and can be found on the websites of the IPS, in other regions this information is not disclosed to the public. For example, in Russia, the IRF is publicly available only for MasterCard, while Visa rates are only available to its members and are subject to a Non-Disclosure Agreement. The average Visa and MasterCard IFR for Russia when using 3-D Secure protocol is 1.7%.

MasterCard Worldwide

MasterCard Intra-Country Interchange Fees

Russia

MCC Group: General

MasterCard Consumer Card Interchange Fees

Fee Tier	MasterCard Consumer Standard, MasterCard Electronic, MasterCard Prepaid Consumer, MasterCard Debit	MasterCard Gold	MasterCard Platinum	MasterCard World	MasterCard World Signia
Low Value Payment (1)	n/a	n/a	n/a	n/a	n/a
Mobile Initiated Top-Up	n/a	n/a	n/a	n/a	n/a
PayPass Terminal	1.30%	1.35%	1.88%	2.00%	2.00%
PayPass (1)	1.50%	1.55%	1.96%	2.10%	2.10%
Chip Terminal	1.40%	1.45%	1.96%	2.10%	2.10%
Full Chip	1.50%	1.55%	1.96%	2.10%	2.10%
Chip Card	1.60%	1.65%	1.96%	2.10%	2.10%
Enhanced Electronic	1.50%	1.55%	1.96%	2.10%	2.10%
Merchant UCAF	1.10%	1.15%	1.58%	1.70%	1.70%
Full UCAF	1.20%	1.25%	1.68%	1.80%	1.80%
Base	1.70%	1.75%	2.00%	2.10%	2.10%
Mobile Payment - Acquirer Domain	1.10%	1.15%	1.56%	1.70%	1.70%
Mobile Payment - Issuer Domain	1.20%	1.25%	1.66%	1.80%	1.80%

MasterCard Commercial Card Interchange Fees

Fee Tier	MasterCard Corporate, MasterCard Electronic Corporate	MasterCard Business, MasterCard Electronic BusinessCard, MasterCard Prepaid Commercial, MasterCard Professional Card
Low Value Payment (1)	n/a	n/a
Mobile Initiated Top-Up	n/a	n/a
PayPass Terminal	1.75%	1.65%
PayPass (1)	1.95%	1.85%
Chip Terminal	1.85%	1.75%
Full Chip	1.95%	1.85%
Chip Card	2.05%	1.95%
Enhanced Electronic	1.95%	1.85%
Merchant UCAF	1.55%	1.45%
Full UCAF	1.65%	1.55%
Base	2.15%	2.05%
Mobile Payment - Acquirer Domain	1.55%	1.45%
Mobile Payment - Issuer Domain	1.65%	1.55%

As an example, let's look at the IRF of MasterCard in Russia (in most of the EU states the IRF is set at around 0.2-03%, which we will discuss later).

Full document is available at:https://www.mastercard.com/us/wce/PDF/Russia.pdf

This document shows the internal IRF rates for Russia. The rates may vary for different MCC groups. In this example, we are looking at a generic MCC group (it includes everything that does not fall into specific MCC categories, which we'll talk about later).

IRF varies for different types of cards: Standard, Gold, Premium. The more privileges a card is giving to its owner, the higher is the IRF rate.

Consumer cards is another name for debit cards, and credit

cards are also called commercial cards. The IRF rates for commercial cards are higher.

Rates vary for different transaction types. Full UCAF stands for a transaction on the Internet, in which both the acquirer and the issuer support 3-D Secure protocol. Merchant UCAF stands for a situation when the acquirer supports 3D-Secure, and the issuer does not. It should be noted that MasterCard encourages the support of 3D-Secure by the issuer with favorable IRF rates. Transactions performed without the use of 3 DS fall into Base category. For example, the IRF rate for MasterCard Standard with full support of 3-D Secure (both by acquirer and by issuer) will be 1.2%, and the IRF on a transaction with the same card but without 3-D Secure will be 1.7%

As we have seen, the IRF rates vary depending on the region and jurisdiction. More specifically, the IRF depends on the location of the acquirer and the issuer. There are local, intra-regional and interregional IRF rates:

- Local (domestic/intra-country) rates apply when both acquirer and issuer are in the same country.
- Intraregional rates apply when both acquirer and issuer are located within the same region.
- Interregional rates apply when acquirer and issuer belong to different regions.

Cross-border transactions are those that cross the borders of one or more countries.

According to Visa classification, the world is divided into 6 regions.

- AP Region — Asia Pacific Region (including Australia and New Zealand);
- Canada Region
- CEMEA Region — Central and Eastern Europe, Middle East and Africa;
- Visa Europe — European Union;
- Latin America and Caribbean Region (LAC Region)
- US Region

MasterCard International divides the world into 5 regions:

- Asia Pacific Region;

- North American Region
- European, Middle-Eastern and African Region;
- Latin American Region;
- Caribbean Region.

The European Region is subdivided into Eastern and Western Europe. For example. a transaction on a Russian card through an aquirer in Iceland will be inter-regional for two regions are involved: Eastern and Western Europe.

Even the acquiring banks quite often do not know the average value of interchange fee as it depends on many factors. It is only at the end of month that the IPS sends out to the acquiring bank a file with all the commissions listed.

In other words, there is a set of IRF rates for every region (and inter-regional exchange). In most cases, the IPS tries to adhere to a single rule: rates are to be lower if the acquirer and the issuer are within the same country. That is why many large online stores open their representative offices in the countries of their main market focus.

The European Union is an exception to this rule. In March 2015, the European Parliament voted for lowering the IRF rates for cross-border transactions between EU member states to 0.2% for debit cards and 0.3% for credit cards (excluding business cards). This decision was the result of many years of negotiations with MasterCard.

The fact is that the EU Regulation No. 924/2009 states that the value of all transactions made in euros should be the same both for local transactions within the territory of one of the EU members and for cross-border transactions between EU member-states.

Let's say that the internal IRF for UK is 0.7%, and the IRF between UK and France is 1.8%. Which means, that a British acquirer will either have to set the rate slightly above 0.7% and operate at a loss when accepting cards issued in France, or set it slightly above 1.8% and fail competition within its own country.

6.4. Industry-specific interchange

In addition to regions and types of cards, the IRF depends on the nature of goods or services provided by the merchant. Thus, IRF is not charged when paying taxes (0%), payments for housing services or for air tickets are subject to significantly lower rates than for goods and services. In other words, the IRF rates vary depend on the MCC code, which is clearly seen in the above document (full version).

6.5. Fees

For each IRF list, there is a set of IPS fees for various operations. It should be noted that the IPS charge both the acquirer for authorization and the issuer for various operations.

The IPS rates are rather low, they can be as low as a few basis points of the total amount for authorization. Their distinctive feature is that authorization fees are fixed and bound to the amount and the number of transactions. In most cases, information about the size of fees is classified, and the rules of the IPS prevent acquirers from disclosing them to third parties.

6.6. Interchange plus

Interchange plus is a pricing model where fixed extra charges are added to the IRF published by Visa and MasterCard. This information gives merchants an understanding of their payment traffic, and also helps them to lower the cost of payments.

Interchange plus practice is most common in the US.

6.7. Surcharge

Surcharge is an additional fee charged by the merchant for accepting bank cards to cover the cost of card transactions. Maximum size of surcharge and acceptance of payment rules are regulated by the IPS and local law.

6.8. Conclusion

In order to determine the real cost of a transaction, you need to know:
- the location of both the acquirer and the issuer;
- type of card (Classic, Premium, etc.);

- whether it is debit card or credit card;
- type of transaction (online with 3 DS, without 3 DS, by phone, etc.);
- MCC of the merchant;
- in some cases you also have to know merchant's turnover.

Based on the location of the acquirer and the issuer, corresponding lists of IRF and fees are selected.

In practice, most banks provide an approximate rate for acquiring, based on the average IRF, which is usually 70-80% of this rate.

Self-control questions

1. What are the components of an Internet payment?
2. Give an example of fixed rate commissions.
3. What is a decline fee? What is a chargeback fee? When are they usually applied?
4. What is IRF? What is its function?
5. What are factors that affect the amount of IRF for a particular transaction.
6. Can an Interchange Fee be equal to zero? If yes, give an example.
7. Why do most acquirers demand zero authorization?
8. What is interchange plus?
9. What is surcharge?
10. Which two lists of commissions determine the cost of payment?

PART FOUR

High-Risk Processing

1. History of the term

Banks and credit card associations label merchants as High-Risk if they pose an increased risk of fraud and chargebacks. Falling into this category are: tourism industry, because holidaymakers often change their plans and return their tickets and vouchers; various dating sites that are selling some quite abstract services, which means that in the case of protested payments merchants had to prove that the requested service was actually provided to the client; bookmakers and casinos that offer quite intangible services to gamblers. High-Risk label is very often applied to semi-legal or illegal types of business.

In the early 2000s, there were many semi-legal merchants that skillfully made advantage of the different laws and interpretations in different countries. A classic example of that is Indian regulation regarding the production of generic medicines (a medicine that works in the same way and provides the same clinical benefit as its brand-name version) with no regard for patents. A new merchant registration with MCC 5912 "Drug Stores, Pharmacies" was a problematic, yet quite feasible. This resulted in generic medicines being mailed all over the world, despite the fact that the laws in many countries make it illegal to import drugs that do not have a local license. There used to exist an entire industry trading in Spyware, programs that pretended to be antivirus software but were actually aimed at gathering information about people or organizations without their knowledge. The number of chargebacks for such merchant activities exceeded all conceivable limits. Call-centers for technical support used to be a common type of fraud. Users' computer would be remotely meddled with to create problems, forcing them to seek advice at technical support, the services being paid by card. In the past few years, we've seen a quite a few dating sites illegally subscribing user's cards and regularly charging money from them.

After the adoption of the Patriot Act in the US, the financial system of the whole world had fundamentally changed. Visa and MasterCard began to tighten their rules for High-Risk categories.

2. Visa Global Brand Protection Program

In June 2011, Visa introduced its new concept of High-Brand Risk merchants. This was preceded by repeated attacks from the media on such dubious business sectors as Indian pharmaceuticals, spyware, tobacco products, etc., which eventually prompted Visa to abandon the previous interpretation of the notion of high-risk business and expand this category with a new list of categories. Ever since, the registration of such merchants in payment systems takes place only after the approval of Visa itself. Illegal registration of such merchants and misappropriation of MCC (miscoding) is punished with huge fines and weighty sanctions. This way Visa is minimizing the risk of accepting payments from companies that engage in illegal activities.

MasterCard launched a similar program in 2005, aiming to protect its participants from illegal business activities, which negatively affects the brand reputation. From that moment on, in many controversial situations, MasterCard a priori interpreted dubious transactions as threatening its brand reputation.

3. Visa Rules

3.1. Visa Global Brand Protection Program
Effective 1 June 2011

3.2. Requirements for all Visa Europe acquirers
All Visa Europe acquirers in the payment system must **not** use the Visa-owned marks:

- In any manner that may bring the Visa-owned marks or Visa Europe or its affiliates into disrepute.
- For the sale or purchase of illegal goods or services.
- In relation to, or for the purchase or trade of, photographs, video imagery, computer-generated images, cartoons, simulation of any other media or activities including, but not limited to:
  - Child pornography
  - Bestiality
  - Rape (or any other non-consensual sexual behavior)

3.3. What is High-Brand Risk?
Effective 1 June 2011, a merchant required to use one of the following MCCs, as amended from time to time, is considered high-brand risk (the list is periodically updated):

- 5962, "Direct Marketing-Travel-Related Arrangement Services"
- 5966, "Direct Marketing-Outbound Telemarketing Merchants" and 5967, "Direct Marketing-Inbound Telemarketing Merchants"
- 7995, "Betting, including Lottery Tickets, Casino Gaming Chips, Off-Track Betting, and Wagers at Race Tracks"
- 5912, "Drug Stores, Pharmacies" and 5122, "Drugs, Drug Proprietaries, Druggist Sundries"

Summary of acquirer risk responsibilities

1. Acquirers must: Implement policies that include the minimum standards established by Visa Europe to mitigate

risk to the payment system. The policies must be approved by the member's Board of Directors or an appropriate senior oversight committee. Be made available to Visa Europe upon request.
2. Control high-risk merchant approval. Utilise merchant agreements that meet Visa Europe minimum requirements for disclosure and clearly define both acquirer and merchant obligations. Ensure that any third party merchant agreements are reviewed and approved prior to their use. Include in the contract with merchants/agents clauses to allow termination of contract if merchants/agents participate in any activity that would harm the Visa brand. Include in the contract with merchants/agents clauses to allow a member, Visa Europe, or its designees, to conduct an onsite review for compliance purposes.
3. Have adequate controls to monitor agent and high-brand risk merchant activity to ensure compliance with Visa Europe requirements and prevent harm to the payment system.
4. Participate in the Visa Merchant Alert Service (VMAS) (unless prohibited by domestic legislation) and ensure that all merchants terminated 'for cause' are listed on VMAS. Request information about a merchant through VMAS prior to signing a merchant agreement.
5. Provide merchants and agents with the necessary education and training. Ensure merchants and agents are aware of the member's policies and guidelines and remain in compliance.

4. Visa Core Rules and Visa Product and Service Rules

https://usa.visa.com/dam/VCOM/download/about-visa/visa-rules-public.pdf

Following are extracts from the Visa Core Rules that apply to all Visa system participants classified in category High-Brand Risk.

1.10.2 Brand Protection.

1.10.2.1 Acquirer Brand Protection Requirements.

An Acquirer must both:

- Ensure that a Merchant, Payment Facilitator, or Sponsored Merchant does not accept Visa Cards for, or display a Visa-Owned Mark on a website that is used in relation to, the purchase or trade of photographs, video imagery, computer-generated images, cartoons, simulation, or any other media or activities including, but not limited to, activities listed in Section 12.7.8.1, "Global Brand Protection Program Non-Compliance Assessments for Illegal or Prohibited Transactions"
- Within 7 calendar days of Notification from Visa, correct the violation or, if requested by Visa, terminate a Merchant, Payment Facilitator, High-Brand Risk Merchant, or High-Risk Internet Payment Facilitator, or require the Payment Facilitator or High-Risk Internet Payment Facilitator to terminate its agreement with the Sponsored Merchant or High-Brand Risk Sponsored Merchant that is in violation

1.10.2.2 Global Brand Protection Program – Requests for Information.

An Acquirer must provide information relating to any request for information presented by Visa, its designees, or any regulatory agency, as required under the Global Brand Protection Program. The Acquirer must provide the required information in writing as soon as possible, but no later than 7 business days following receipt of the request for information.

1.10.5 High-Brand Risk Merchants

1.10.5.1 High-Brand Risk Acquirer Requirements.

An Acquirer of High-Brand Risk Merchants, High-Risk Internet Payment Facilitators, or High-Brand Risk Sponsored Merchants must do all of the following:

- Participate in the Visa Merchant Trace System (VMTS), where available and permitted under applicable laws or regulations, and both:
- Query VMTS before entering into an agreement with a prospective Electronic Commerce Merchant or Mail/Phone Order Merchant or Sponsored Merchant
- List any Electronic Commerce Merchant or Mail/Phone

Order Merchant or Sponsored Merchant that has been terminated for just cause on VMTS
- Provide Visa with a suspect violation report if a Merchant or Agent is identified by the Member as processing illegal or prohibited Transactions.

Visa may waive or suspend non-compliance assessments to accommodate unique or extenuating circumstances or if violations of the Visa Rules are identified and rectified before receipt of formal Notification from Visa that a violation has occurred.

1.10.5.2 High-Brand Risk Acquirer Requirements.

An Acquirer that has not previously acquired Transactions from Electronic Commerce Merchants, Mail/ Phone Order Merchants, or Sponsored Merchants classified as high-brand risk must both:

- Be financially sound (as determined by Visa)
- Be rated above-standard (a Visa Member risk rating of "A" or "B") and meet a minimum equity requirement of USD 100 million[15]

5.3.1.3 Acquirer Responsibilities Regarding Payment Facilitators.

Acquirers must comply with all of the following:

- Ensure that its registration of its Payment Facilitator, including the name the Payment Facilitator uses to identify itself in the Merchant name field and the attestation of due diligence review, is confirmed by Visa before submitting Transactions on behalf of the Payment Facilitator or its Sponsored Merchant. If the Payment Facilitator is considered to be high-brand risk, it must be registered as a High-Risk Internet Payment Facilitator even if that Payment Facilitator has previously been registered with Visa.

10.1.2 Electronic Commerce Merchant Requirements

10.1.2.1 Yearly Review of Electronic Commerce Merchant

At least once each year, a US Acquirer must examine its Electronic Commerce Merchant's website and conduct an enhanced due diligence review, as specified in Section

1.5.1.2, "Merchant Qualification Standards", if any of the following applies:

- The Electronic Commerce Merchant or Sponsored Merchant is required to be classified with an MCC considered by Visa to be high-brand risk
- The Merchant is identified by any Visa Chargeback monitoring program or designated at any time as an identified Merchant by the Risk Identification Service Online
- The Acquirer becomes aware the Merchant is selling products or services that were not documented in the Merchant Agreement or disclosed in the Merchant's business description

The Acquirer conducts a periodic review of the Merchant as required by its internal procedures

10.1.2.2 Electronic Commerce Transaction Type Prohibition.

A Merchant, Payment Facilitator, Sponsored Merchant, or entity classified as high-brand risk, as specified in Section 10.5.6.1, "High-Brand Risk MCCs," that displays a Visa-Owned Mark on its website must not accept Cards for the purchase or trade of photographs, video imagery, computer-generated images, cartoons, simulation, or any other media or activities, as specified in Section 10.6, "Brand Protection."

Violation of this requirement may result in the termination of the Merchant, Payment Facilitator, Sponsored Merchant, High-Brand Risk Merchant, High-Risk Internet Payment Facilitator, or High-Brand Risk Sponsored Merchant.

10.2.2.9 High-Risk Agent Registration

An Acquirer that signs an Agent to solicit High-Brand Risk Merchants must register that Agent as high-risk with Visa.

10.5.1.3 Acquirer Monitoring of Payment Facilitator and Sponsored Merchant Activity

An Acquirer must comply with Merchant monitoring standards for each of its Payment Facilitators, as specified in Section 10.5.7, "High-Brand Risk Merchant Monitoring."

A Sponsored Merchant that exceeds Visa thresholds for excessive Chargebacks or Fraud Activity will be subject to monitoring programs.

10.5.6 High-Brand Risk Merchants

10.5.6.1 High-Brand Risk MCCs

A Merchant required to use one of the following MCCs is considered a High-Brand Risk Merchant:

- 5962 (Direct Marketing – Travel-Related Arrangement Services)
- 5966 (Direct Marketing – Outbound Telemarketing Merchants) and 5967 (Direct Marketing – Inbound Telemarketing Merchants)
- 7995 (Betting, including Lottery Tickets, Casino Gaming Chips, Off-Track Betting, and Wagers at Race Tracks)
- 5912 (Drug Stores, Pharmacies) and 5122 (Drugs, Drug Proprietaries, Druggist Sundries)
- 5993 (Cigar Stores and Stands), for Merchants that sell cigarettes in a Card-Absent Environment

10.5.6.2 High-Brand Risk Merchant Registration

Before accepting Transactions from a High-Brand Risk Merchant, a US Acquirer must register the Merchant using a Visa U.S.A. High Risk Merchant Registration and Certification form.

10.5.7 High-Brand Risk Merchant Monitoring

An Acquirer should monitor the activity of its High-Brand Risk Merchants and Payment Facilitators.

Also, an Acquirer of a High-Risk Internet Payment Facilitator must:

- Register its High-Brand Risk Sponsored Merchants as High-Brand Risk Merchants
- Monitor its High-Risk Internet Payment Facilitators

10.5.7.2 High-Brand Risk Merchant Unusual Activity Reporting

For its High-Brand Risk Merchants, a US Acquirer must generate unusual activity reports daily, and report any unusual activity to Visa within 2 business days, if either of the following:

- Current weekly gross sales volume equals or exceeds USD 5,000 and any of the following exceeds 150% of the normal daily activity
- Number of daily Transaction Receipt Deposits
- Gross amount of daily Deposits
- Average Transaction amount
- Number of daily Chargebacks
- Average elapsed time between the Transaction Date and Processing Date for a Transaction (counting each as one day) exceeds 15 calendar days

10.5.7.3 High-Brand Risk Merchants – Acquirer Requirements

For a High-Brand Risk Merchant, an Acquirer must do all of the following:

- Retain at least the following daily data:
- Gross sales volume
- Average Transaction amount
- Number of Transaction Receipts
- Average elapsed time between the Transaction Date of the Transaction Receipt and the Settlement Date (counting each as one day)
- Number of Chargebacks
- Collect the data over a period of at least one month, beginning after each Merchant's initial Deposit
- Use the data to determine the Merchant's normal daily activity of the categories specified in this section
- Begin the daily monitoring of the Merchant's activity processed on the 31st calendar day from the first Deposit
- Compare current related data to the normal daily activity parameters at least daily
- Review the Merchant's normal daily activity at least weekly, using the previous week's activity
- At least monthly, adjust the Merchant's normal daily activity, using the previous month's activity

10.5.7.5 Investigation of Merchant on High-Brand Risk Merchant Exception Report

An Acquirer must investigate a Merchant that appears on its High-Brand Risk Merchant exception report within one business day of generating the report. If the investigation reveals Merchant involvement in illegal or fraudulent activity, the Acquirer must do all of the following:

- Take appropriate legal action to minimize losses
- Cooperate with Issuers and law enforcement agencies
- Attempt to make the Merchant responsible for the Transaction
- Hold funds, if possible
- Initiate criminal and civil proceedings against the Merchant, if applicable

10.5.7.6 Acquirer Provision of High-Brand Risk Merchant Monitoring Information

Upon Visa request, an Acquirer must provide both of the following within 7 calendar days to demonstrate compliance with High-Brand Risk Merchant monitoring standards:

- Copies of actual reports or records used to monitor the Merchant's Deposits
- Any other data requested by Visa

10.5.7.7 High-Brand Risk Chargeback Monitoring Program

Visa monitors the total volume of US Domestic Interchange, International Interchange, and Chargebacks for a US Merchant specified in Section 10.5.6.1, "High-Brand Risk MCCs," and identifies Merchants that experience all of the following activity levels during any month:

* 100 or more interchange Transactions

* 100 or more Chargebacks

* A 1% or higher ratio of overall Chargeback-to-Interchange volume

For the purposes of the High-Brand Risk Chargeback Monitoring Program, if a Merchant submits Interchange under multiple names, Visa:

- Groups the Merchant activity
- Notifies the respective Acquirer of the Interchange

grouping

10.5.7.8 High-Brand Risk Chargeback Monitoring Program – Chargeback Ratios

If a Merchant specified in Section 10.5.6.1, "High-Brand Risk MCCs," meets or exceeds either of the applicable Chargeback ratios specified in Section 10.5.7.7, "High-Brand Risk Chargeback Monitoring Program – US Region," Visa sends a Notification to the Merchant's Acquirer.

Within 15 calendar days of receipt of the Notification, the Acquirer must:

- Notify the Merchant
- Provide Visa with the specific information requested

10.5.7.9 Merchant Disqualification from the Visa Program

Visa may disqualify a US Merchant specified in Section 10.5.6.1, "High-Brand Risk MCCs," from participating in the Visa Program if the Merchant does any of the following:

- Meets or exceeds a critical level of Chargeback activity
- Acts with the intent to circumvent Visa programs
- Causes harm to the Visa system

Visa will send a Notification to the Acquirer advising all of the following:

- The date the Acquirer must stop submitting the disqualified Merchant's Transactions
- Reasons for the disqualification
- Notice of the right to appeal

The Acquirer may appeal the disqualification as follows:

- The Acquirer's appeal letter must be received by Visa within 15 days of the Acquirer's receipt of the disqualification Notification.
- The Acquirer must pay a non-refundable fee and include it with the appeal letter.
- The evidence and arguments for the appeal must be submitted in the appeal letter.
- No oral presentations are permitted.

10.5.8 High-Risk Internet Payment Facilitator Requirements

10.5.8.1 High-Brand Risk Acquirer Registration

An Acquirer that has not previously acquired Electronic Commerce Merchants or Mail/Phone Order Merchants classified by Visa as High-Brand Risk Merchants must:

- Submit to Visa a Visa New High-Brand Risk Acquirer Registration Form
- Not process or enter a High-Brand Risk Transaction into Interchange until written confirmation has been received from Visa that the Acquirer has been registered and approved by Visa

10.5.8.2 High-Risk Internet Payment Facilitator Agreement

An Acquirer must ensure that a High-Risk Internet Payment Facilitator Agreement requires both:

- That the High-Brand Risk Sponsored Merchant Agreement be signed by a senior officer of the High-Risk Internet Payment Facilitator
- The High-Risk Internet Payment Facilitator to report both:
  - Acquisition of new High-Brand Risk Sponsored Merchants
  - Monthly Transaction activity for all High-Brand Risk Sponsored Merchants.

The reports must be provided to Visa in Visa-specified electronic formats.

10.5.8.4 High-Risk Internet Payment Facilitator Processing Requirements.

If a Cardholder accesses the Website of an electronic commerce High-Brand Risk Merchant or a High- Brand Risk Sponsored Merchant and is then linked to the Website of the High-Risk Internet Payment Facilitator for payment, the name of the High-Risk Internet Payment Facilitator must appear in the Authorization Request and Clearing Record in conjunction with the name of the High-Brand Risk Sponsored Merchant.

10.5.8.5 Visa Right to Prohibit or Disqualify Sponsored Merchants.

Visa may require a US Acquirer to directly contract with a Sponsored Merchant if the Sponsored Merchant either:

- Generates or has a history of generating excessive levels of exception items (Chargebacks and/or credits) within a 12-month period
- Takes action to evade responsibility for compliance with the Visa Rules

Visa may disqualify a High-Risk Internet Payment Facilitator or High-Brand Risk Sponsored Merchant in accordance with the High-Risk Chargeback Monitoring Program or for other activity that causes undue harm to the Visa system

10.6 Brand Protection.

10.6.1 Global Brand Protection Program

10.6.1.1 Global Brand Protection Program Data Quality

To enable the valid identification of data for the Global Brand Protection Program, an Acquirer must correctly classify its High-Brand Risk Merchants.

If Visa determines that an Acquirer or its Merchant changed, modified, or altered the Merchant name or Merchant data in any way to circumvent the Global Brand Protection Program, Visa may:

- Assess a non-compliance assessment
- Require the Acquirer to implement risk reduction measures
- Prohibit the Acquirer from acquiring High-Brand Risk Merchants for a period of one year or more

10.6.1.2 Annual Assessments

An Acquirer is subject to an annual assessment to ensure compliance with the Global Brand Protection Program and the Visa Rules if either of the following:

- All of the following quarterly thresholds, as amended from time to time, are met or exceeded:
    - A minimum of 10,000 International Transactions in a Card-Absent Environment classified as High-Brand Risk Transactions
    - USD 1,000,000 worth of International Transactions

in a Card-Absent Environment classified as High-Brand Risk Transactions
- A ratio of 10% of International Transactions in a Card-Absent Environment classified as High-Brand Risk Transactions versus all International Transactions acquired in a Card-Absent Environment
- One or more Merchants is identified under the Global Brand Protection Program as having been involved in illegal or prohibited Transactions

12.3.2 High-Risk Internet Payment Facilitator Non-Compliance Assessments

12.3.2.1 High-Risk Internet Payment Facilitator Registration Non-Compliance Assessments.

An Acquirer that fails to comply with the registration program requirements for High-Risk Internet Payment Facilitators is subject to a non-compliance assessment, as follows:

- USD 25,000 per month per High-Brand Risk Sponsored Merchant or High-Risk Internet Payment Facilitator
- After 3 violations in a calendar year, one or both of the following:
  - USD 100,000 for each 30-calendar-day period of non-compliance
  - Prohibition against signing High-Brand-Risk Sponsored Merchants

12.5.1.1 Online Gambling Transaction Identification Non-Compliance Assessment.

An Acquirer is subject to the non-compliance assessments specified in Section 12.7.8, "Global Brand Protection Program Non-Compliance Assessments," if an Authorization Request for an Online Gambling Transaction contains incorrect data or fails to include all of the following:

- An appropriate MCC to identify the High-Brand Risk Merchant, as specified in Section 10.5.6.1, "High-Brand Risk MCCs"
- MCC 7995 (Betting), for an Online Gambling Transaction,

as specified in Section 5.9.3.6, "Online Gambling Merchant Requirements"
- POS Condition Code 59

12.7.5.1 High-Brand Risk Acquirer Registration Non-Compliance Assessments.

If Visa determines that an Acquirer that previously did not acquire High-Brand Risk Transactions in a Card-Absent Environment has failed to comply with the registration requirements specified in Section 10.5.8.1, "High-Brand Risk Acquirer Registration," Visa may impose a non-compliance assessment of USD 25,000 to the Acquirer per calendar month of non-compliance. Continued non-compliance may result in Visa prohibiting that Acquirer from acquiring High-Brand Risk Merchants.

12.7.9 High-Brand Risk Merchant Monitoring Non-Compliance Assessments

12.7.9.1 Global Merchant Chargeback Monitoring Program – High-Brand Risk Merchants – Non-Compliance Assessments

Table 12-18, "High-Brand Risk Merchants in the Global Merchant Chargeback Monitoring Program – Acquirer Fees and Non-Compliance Assessments," and the applicable Fee Schedule specify the fees and non-compliance assessments per international Chargeback for Acquirers of High-Brand Risk Merchants placed in the Global Merchant Chargeback Monitoring Program.

Event	Month	Visa Action, Fee, or Non-Compliance Assessment
Merchant meets or exceeds the specified Chargeback ratio (*)	Months 1-3	Fee per Chargeback per month for each identified Merchant Outlet (**)
Merchant meets or exceeds the specified	Months	Fee per Chargeback per month for each

Chargeback ratio (*)	4-6	identified Merchant Outlet (**)
Merchant meets or exceeds the specified Chargeback ratio (*)	Month 7 and subsequent months	Fee per Chargeback per month for each identified Merchant Outlet (**) and Visa may disqualify the Merchant from participation in the Visa Program
Merchant meets or exceeds the specified Chargeback ratio (*) without an effective Chargeback reduction plan, and 2 of the following levels of Chargeback activity are reached: • Merchant's Chargeback ratio is 2 or more times the specified Chargeback ratio • Merchant is assessed fees for 3,000 or more Chargebacks • Merchant is assessed US $1 million or more in Global Merchant Chargeback Monitoring Program fees	Single month Single month When reached	Visa may disqualify the Merchant from participation in the Visa Program
Acquirer does not	When	USD 25,000 per

| identify a High-Brand Risk Merchant with the correct MCC, as specified in Section 10.5.6.1, "High-Brand Risk MCCs" | violation occurs | Merchant per month |

(*) The Chargeback ratio threshold is 2%.

(**) If the Acquirer and Merchant have not implemented procedures to reduce Chargebacks, Visa may impose on the Acquirer a non-compliance assessment of USD 200 for each international Chargeback received for its Merchant.

Basic concepts:
- Some of the MCCs refer exclusively to High-Risk category.
- Every new Acquirer for High-Brand Risk merchants must complete Visa registration procedure. There is a list of criteria that an Acquirer must match. Certain restrictions are applied to acquirers that had previously cooperated with High-Brand Risk merchants.
- Payment Faciliators working with High-Brand Risk merchants should be submitted by Acquirer to Visa for registration.
- Acquirer should constantly monitor the activity of its High-Brand Risk agents and merchants to ensure that the payment system is not compromised by illegal or fraudulent transactions.
- There is is established list of merchant activities, for which transactions are to be denied.
- Acquirer can not service High-Risk Brand merchant before receiving a written permission from Visa.
- There is a system of penalties for non-compliance with the program, which also establishes acquirer's obligations in assisting with investigation of merchant's illegal activities.

5. MasterCard Rules

5.1. Business Risk Assessment and Mitigation (BRAM) Program

MasterCard Standards require customers to comply with all applicable laws and not to engage in illegal behavior, or in behavior that would reflect negatively on MasterCard. MasterCard launched the BRAM Program in 2005 to protect MasterCard, its customers, merchants, and cardholders from activities that may be illegal or could negatively impact the brands of MasterCard, and other stakeholders in the payments network. MasterCard launched the BRAM Monitoring Program (BMP) in 2007.

MasterCard encourages each acquirer to conduct due diligence on each of its merchants and their services on an ongoing basis to determine the legality and legitimacy of the goods or services being offered for sale and the jurisdictions where they are being sold.

The impermissible activities addressed by the BRAM program include, but are not limited to the:

- Illegal sale of drugs on Schedule I of the Controlled Substances Act (CSA), or that are otherwise prohibited by applicable law from being sold
- Illegal sale of prescription drugs
- Illegal sale of tobacco products
- Brand-damaging sale of images of offensive and/or non-consensual adult pornography
- Illegal sale of images of child exploitation
- Facilitation of Internet gambling in jurisdictions where it is illegal
- Sale of counterfeit merchandise
- Sale of goods or services in violation of intellectual property rights
- Sale of illegal electronic devices (such as modification chips and jammers)
- Sale of certain types of drugs or chemicals (such as synthetic drugs, Salvia Divinorum, psilocybin mushrooms and spores, and nitrite inhalants)

- Illegal sale of any other product or service

The products, services, and merchant models mentioned in this article do not represent an exhaustive list of illegal or brand-damaging activities.

Merchant Monitoring Program (MMP)

MasterCard introduced MMP to adapt to new trends and technologies in the industry and to further MasterCard compliance efforts and those of its customers. The new MMP is designed to:

- Encourage acquirers to proactively monitor for and prevent BRAM violations related to content, products, and services.
- Encourage acquirers to proactively monitor for and prevent merchant transaction laundering.[16]
- Create an optional framework to incent transaction laundering detection.
- Permit acquirers to leverage any service provider as a solution for BRAM monitoring and merchant transaction laundering detection services.
- Require acquirers to register their chosen service provider to participate in the MMP.
- Provide potential assessment mitigation for acquirers that register an MMSP for monitoring and detecting BRAM and merchant transaction laundering activity and comply with MMP requirements.

MasterCard reminds acquirers that they are solely responsible for ensuring that their merchants' activity complies fully with MasterCard Standards.

Merchant Monitoring Service Provider

MasterCard has created a new service provider category called an MMSP. Acquirers can voluntarily register MMSPs as a service provider with MasterCard for participation in the MMP. An acquirer may choose a single service provider to provide both BRAM monitoring and merchant transaction laundering detection services, or the acquirer may elect to choose two or more service providers to provide BRAM monitoring and merchant transaction laundering detection services.

If the acquirer chooses to participate in the MMP, the acquirer must register the MMSP or itself along with its internal detection system and comply with all MMP and service provider requirements.

A brief outline of BRAM:

- BRAM is 6 years older than Visa GBPP.
- Like GBPP, BRAM sets a list of prohibited goods and services for which MasterCard disallows to buy.
- BRAM requires acquirers to monitor the activity of their merchants. It introduces a new type of provider, MMSP, for monitoring.
- Mastercard sets conditions for mitigating penalties for acquirers that are using MMSP services.

Self-control questions

1. What does the term High-Risk mean?
2. What is miscoding?
3. Explain the term "affiliate program".
4. What program did Visa introduce in June 2011 for brand protection? What was it introduced for?
5. What is "High-Brand Risk" according to Visa classification?
6. Do online casinos require registration directly with Visa?
7. What is the meaning of the High-Brand Risk Chargeback Monitoring Program? What criteria for it do you know?
8. What penalty does Visa impose on an acquirer that incorrectly identifies High-Brand risk merchant and assigns it a wrong MCC?
9. What is Business Risk Assessment and Mitigation Program?
10. Give a definition for Merchant Monitoring Program.
11. Explain the concept of the Merchant Monitoring Service Provider.

Glossary of terms

3-D Secure (Three-Domain Secure, 3 DS) is a secure protocol designed to be an additional security layer for online credit and debit card transactions, i.e. in card-not-present (CNP) environment. It is designed to ensure enhanced security and strong authentication, to protect the use of debit or credit cards for online purchases. It was first deployed by Visa and eventually the services based on the protocol have also been adopted by other payment systems. Visa's protocol is known as Verified by Visa (VbV), MasterCard's analogue is known as MasterCard SecureCode, and at JCB International it is called J/Secure.

Acquiring is the process of accepting bank cards for payment for goods and services.

Acquirer is a credit institution (usually a bank) engaged in acquiring.

Authorization is the process of validating funds available on a credit or debit card at merchant's request. An authorization request includes transaction risk evaluation, and, if approved, the authorized amount is held in reserve from cardholder's account balance.

Account Funding Transaction (AFT) method pulls funds from a sender's account (card), in preparation for pushing funds to a recipient's account (a financial institution providing money transfer services).

Bitcoin is a decentralized peer-to-peer network and a distributed database using the unit of the same name for accounting operations and a data transfer protocol of the same name. Cryptographic methods are employed for the functioning and protection of the system. All information about transactions between system addresses is available as open source.

Bank account is an account opened by the bank for legal entities or individuals enabling their participation in non-cash turnover of money and accumulation of non-cash funds on it for appropriate use.

Bank is a credit organization that has the exclusive right to carry out all of such operations as accepting funds from individuals and legal entities into deposits, investment of such funds on its own behalf and at its own expense on terms of repayment, payment, urgency, as well as opening and maintaining bank accounts of physical and legal entities, and conducting other transactions.

Billing descriptor is the way a company's name appears on a credit card statement. it is used by the credit card customer to identify who a payment was made to on a particular transaction.

Base I and **Base II** are two phases of the VisaNet system for performing electronic real-time authorization for credit card transactions of Visa members.

BankAmericard is a general-use credit card introduced in 1958 by the Bank of America. The pilot program was a huge success and eventually developed into an independent payment system that changed its name to Visa in 1976.

Bank of America is an American financial conglomerate, which provides a wide range of financial services to individuals and businesses, it's the largest bank holding company in the United States in terms of assets, it ranks 23rd among the largest companies in the world according to Forbes (2015).

Bank Identification Number (BIN) uniquely identifies the institution issuing the card. BIN is the initial four to six numbers that appear on a credit card.

Credit Organization(KO), in accordance with the legislation of the Russian Federation, is a legal entity that, for the purpose of deriving profit as its main objective, and on the basis of a special license from the Central Bank of the Russian Federation, has the right to conduct banking operations stipulated for in the Federal Law "On Banks and banking activities ".

Correspondent account is an account established by a banking institution to receive deposits from, make payments on behalf of, or handle other financial transactions for another financial institution.

China UnionPay is a Chinese payment system. Founded in 2002 as an association for China's banking card industry, it operates under the approval of the State Council and People's Bank of China. Its shareholders include more than 200 financial institutions; the largest of which owns up to 6% of the shares.

Chargeback is the procedure of protesting a transaction initiated by the issuing bank for consumer protection, it results in payment amount being directly debited from the recipient (acquirer bank) and returned to the payer, after which the burden of proof lies with the merchant.

Discount rate is the rate charged to a merchant for payment processing services on debit and credit card transactions

Diners Club International (DCI), founded as **Diners Club**, was the first independent credit card company in the world. Formed on January 28, 1950 by Frank X., McNamara, Alfred Bloomingdale and Ralph Schneider, it established the concept of a self-sufficient company producing credit cards for travel and entertainment.

Emission refers to the issue of bank cards, opening accounts and conducting settlements, as well as cash servicing of clients when they are performing transactions with the use of bank cards. In the book we are concerned only with the emission of bank cards, but in its broad sense this term is applied to securities, banknotes, etc.

Friendly Fraud or Chargeback Fraud refers to a situation when a consumer makes an online shopping purchase with their own credit card, and then requests a chargeback from the issuing bank after receiving the purchased goods or services. When a chargeback occurs, the merchant is accountable, regardless of whatever measures they took to verify the transaction.

High Risk or **High Brand Risk** is a term characterizing the category of merchants with high risk of excessive chargebacks.

Issuer an entity (financial institutions) that issues payment cards.

IPS – International Payment System.

Interbank clearing is a funds transfer network between banks with the purpose of offsetting mutual currency claims between legal entities.

Imprinter is a mechanical device to reproduce the name and account number of a cardholder on a sales slip. It holds a custom plate displaying embossed merchant's data. A plastic card is inserted into the imprinter and a slip is put in, on which an imprint of the identification data of the merchant and the customer's card is made.

Interchange Reimbursement fee (IRF) is a fee paid by financial institutions involved in processing card transactions to each other. Normally it's a fee paid by the merchant's acquirer to the client's issuing bank. However, in some cases the opposite takes place when a payment for an exchange is received by the acquirer from the issuer.

JCB is a major payment system in Japan and one of the top five payment systems in the world. The international name of the company in English is JCB Co., Ltd. It's headquarters are located in Tokyo. It ranks world's third among payment systems for the number of locations accepting cards.

KYC (Know Your Customer) is a term in banking and stock exchange regulation for financial institutions and bookmakers, as well as other companies working with private money, indicating their obligation to verify the identity of their clients and assessing potential risks of illegal intentions before conducting a financial transaction.

Mir payment system is the Russian national payment system. The first Mir cards were issued on December 15, 2015. It is operated by PS Mir, AO "National system of payment cards".

Mutual settlements are actions that discharge obligations in respect of funds transfers between two or more parties of a payment system.

Merchant Identification Number (MID) is a unique number assigned to a merchant account by is aquirer to identify it throughout the course of processing activities.

Merchant Category Code (MCC) is a four-digit number used to classify the business by the type of goods or services it provides.

Merchant Account is a type of bank account that allows businesses to accept payments in multiple ways, typically with debit or credit cards.

Merchant stands for retail business establishment providing goods or services, a key participant in the payment system.

MasterCard Worldwide or **MasterCard Incorporated** is an international payment system, and transnational financial corporation, which brings together 22 thousand financial institutions in 210 countries.

Master Charge is the name adopted in 1969 by Interbank Cards Association (ICA). In 1979, it was renamed to "MasterCard International".

Maestro is a multi-national debit card service owned by Mastercard that was founded in 1992. Maestro cards are obtained from associate banks and can be linked to the card holder's current account, or they can be prepaid cards.

Non-banking Credit Organization (NKO) is a financial institution that has the right to carry out certain banking operations provided for by the Federal Law "On Banks and Banking Activities". Admissible combinations of banking operations for non-banking credit organizations in Russia are established by the Bank of Russia.

National Payment Card System (NSPK) is an operational and payment clearing center for processing transactions on bank cards in the Russian Federation. It is also the operator of the national payment system Mir.

Operations Center is an organization that provides access to money transfer services to participants of a payment system and to their clients, as well as exchange of electronic messages.

Original Credit Transaction (OCT) method credits (pushes) funds to the recipient's Visa account.

Point of Sale (POS) is an organization that accepts bank cards for payment for goods and services. In this book the term is used as a synonym for "merchant".

Payment Clearing House is a common entity (or a common processing mechanism) through which participants agree to exchange transfer instructions for funds.

Payment page is a web page that accepts data (including card data) for the payment of goods and services.

Payment system is any system used to settle financial transactions through the transfer of monetary value, and includes the institutions, instruments, people, rules, procedures, standards, and technologies that make such an exchange possible.

Primary Account Number (PAN) is simply a card number.

PayPal is a major company operating a global online payments system that supports online money transfers, payments for goods and services, and serves as an electronic alternative to traditional paper methods like cheques and money orders.

Payment Service Provider (PSP) offers merchants and banks its online services for accepting electronic payments by a variety of payment methods.

Payment Facilitator is a merchant service provider that simplifies the merchant account enrollment process on behalf of the aquirer. A Payment Facilitator, PayFac for short, is simply a sub-merchant account for a merchant service provider in order to provide payment processing services to their own merchant clients.

Payment Card Industry Data Security Standard (PCI DSS) is an information security standard for organizations that handle branded credit cards from the major card schemes. The PCI Standard is mandated by the card brands and administered by the Payment Card Industry Security Standards Council (PCI SSC) established by international payment systems Visa, MasterCard, American Express, JCB and Discover.

Reversal is a request from the cardholder to the issuing bank to release the reserved amount sent before the actual charge-off from the cardholder's account had occurred. A reversal can be full or partial.

Refund is the transfer of funds from the merchant's account back to the cardholder's bank account. Refunds are always associated with a transaction that has been authorized and settled.

Settlement Center is an organization within a payment system that provides execution of orders for its participants by debiting and crediting funds to their bank accounts, as well as sending confirmations concerning the execution of such orders within the payment system.

SWIFT, The Society for Worldwide Interbank Financial Telecommunications is an international interbank system providing a network that enables financial institutions worldwide to send and receive information about financial transactions in a secure, standardized and reliable environment.

Sponsored Merchant is a merchant that signs a contract with a Payment Facilitator in order to obtain payment services.

Transaction Laundering is a concept introduced by MasterCard that denotes situations where one outlet accepts money in favor of another. Such operations are illegal from the point of view of Visa and MasterCard payment systems.

Terminal Identification Number (TID) is a unique number assigned and tied to a specific point of sale (POS) terminal that can be used to identify the specific location of a transaction.

Visa's Zero Liability is Visa's policy guaranteeing that cardholders are not liable for unauthorized use of their cards. This policy protects cardholders from unauthorized charges. Any funds taken from an account due to fraudulent use will be returned to the owner. This policy only applies to cards issued by US banks.

VISA International Service Association (Visa throughout this book) is an international payment system. Currently, the association includes two companies: Visa Inc. (Foster City, USA), which owns all rights to the trademark and technology used, and Visa Europe Services Inc. (Great Britain, London), which is managed by European banks and operates under a licenses from Visa Inc.

Visa Inc. a US transnational company that provides payment services. It's at the basis of the association of the same name.

Western Union is an American financial services and communications company that specializes in the transfer of money from one location to another. Founded in 1851, it is currently one of the leaders in the international money transfer market.

WebMoney or **WebMoney Transfer** is an electronic settlement system founded in 1998 and owned by WM Transfer Ltd. Legally, the system transfers property rights, the settlement for which is carried out with the use of special accounting units (title units) nominated in relation to different currencies and gold. WebMoney is not registered as an electronic payment system in Russia, since, from the legal point of view, title units are not electronic money.

Yandex.Money is a service of electronic payments for the Russian segment of the Internet. It allows accepting payments by electronic money, cash, and bank cards.

Notes

[1] Chargeback (payment return) – the procedure of protesting a transaction initiated by the issuing bank for consumer protection, it results in payment amount being directly debited from the recipient (acquirer bank) and returned to the payer, after which the burden of proof lies with the merchant.

[2] ISS (Internet Information Services) – a proprietary set of servers for a number of Internet services from Microsoft. IIS is distributed with the operating systems of Windows NT family.

[3] Keylogger – software or hardware device that records various user actions, such as keystrokes on computer keyboard, mouse movement and clicks etc.

[4] Level 1 Merchants (according to Visa and MasterCard classification) are trade and service enterprises that process, store or transmit data on 6 million or more transactions per year, or service providers (processing centers, payment gateways etc), processing, storing or trans

[5] Imprinter is a mechanical device that reproduces the name and account number of a cardholder on a sales slip. It holds a custom plate displaying embossed merchant's data. A plastic card is inserted into the imprinter and a slip is put in, on which an imprint of the identification data of the merchant and the customer's card is made.

[6] Xapo is one of Bitcoin's online wallets.

[7] Floor limit - historically, this term denotes the amount set by the IPS, above which transactions on cards had to undergo mandatory authorization. Ever since payments on cards began to be processed electronically and all transactions processed online, the requirements for such limits had become merely formal and today the term is rarely used.

[8] In peer-to-peer network all computers are equal, there is no hierarchy among them and no dedicated central server. As a rule, each computer functions both as client and as server; in other words, there no single computer is responsible for administering the entire network.

[9] For a complete list of countries in the region, see the Visa rules.

[10] Does not apply to issuers of Visa Electron.

[11] International Airline Program – special conditions of acquiring for international airlines established by Visa in 1992, in particular, they provide special (usually lower) Interchange Fees, as well as the permission for cross-border-acquiring.

[12] Merchant or Sponsored Merchant who works at his place of domicile must include the city, state/province and country of his personal residence, but is not required to provide a full and accurate residence address.

[13] An electronic receipt is requested for transactions conducted in the field of electronic commerce. The acquiring bank must provide such a receipt within 30 days.

[14] Late Presentment – an established term denoting situations involving a significant delay in transactions processing

[15] Visa can waive these claims in exchange for guarantees and evidence of risk management at a level that meets Visa standards. In particular, it can be about additional collateral on Visa accounts.

[16] Merchant Transaction Laundering is when a merchant processes card transactions on behalf of another merchant (also referred to as factoring or transaction aggregation). Transaction laundering may serve as reason for establishing a fact of a BRAM nonconformity and imposing penalties for non-compliance with MasterCard standards, such as registering an incorrect MCC (miscoding) or not registering as a high-risk merchant in MasterCard Registration Program (MRP).

Printed in Great Britain
by Amazon